TEENAGE COUPLES

EXPECTATIONS
AND REALITY

Other Books by Jeanne Warren Lindsay:

Teenage Couples—Caring, Commitment and Change:
How to Build a Relationship that Lasts
Teenage Couples—Coping with Reality: Dealing with Money,
In-Laws, Babies and Other Details of Daily Life
Teens Parenting—Your Baby's First Year
Teens Parenting—The Challenge of Toddlers
Teen Dads: Rights, Responsibilities and Joys
Do I Have a Daddy? A Story About a Single-Parent Child
School-Age Parents: Challenge of Three-Generation Living
Parents, Pregnant Teens and the Adoption Option
Pregnant Too Soon: Adoption Is an Option
Open Adoption: A Caring Option

By Jeanne Lindsay and Jean Brunelli:

Teens Parenting—Your Pregnancy and Newborn Journey
(Available in "regular" [RL 6],
Easier Reading [RL 3], and Spanish editions.)

By Jeanne Lindsay and Sally McCullough:

Teens Parenting—Discipline from Birth to Three

By Jeanne Lindsay and Sharon Rodine:

Teen Pregnancy Challenge, Book One: Strategies for Change
Teen Pregnancy Challenge, Book Two: Programs for Kids

By Jeanne Lindsay and Catherine Monserrat:

Adoption Awareness: A Guide for Teachers,
Counselors, Nurses and Caring Others

TEENAGE COUPLES
Expectations
and
Reality

Teen Views on Living Together, Roles, Work, Jealousy, and Partner Abuse

Jeanne Warren Lindsay, MA, CFCS

Morning Glory Press

Buena Park, California

Teenage Couples Series for Students:
*Teenage Couples—Caring, Commitment and Change:
How to Build a Relationship that Lasts*
and
*Teenage Couples—Coping with Reality: Dealing with Money,
In-Laws, Babies and Other Details of Daily Life*
with workbooks and curriculum guide

Library of Congress Cataloging-in-Publication Data
Lindsay, Jeanne Warren.
    Teenage couples. Expectations and reality : teen views on living
together, roles, work, jealousy, and partner abuse / Jeanne Warren
Lindsay.
        p. cm.
    Includes bibliographical references and index.
    ISBN 0-930934-98-9 (pbk.). -- ISBN 0-930934-99-7 (hardcover)
    1. Teenage marriage--United States. 2. Unmarried couples--
United States. 3. Teenagers--United States--Attitudes.   I. Title.
HQ799.2.M3L557   1996
306.81'0835--dc20   95-46209
                                                                CIP

MORNING GLORY PRESS, INC.
6595 San Haroldo Way   Buena Park, CA 90620-3748
        (714) 828-1998   FAX (714) 828-2049
        Printed and bound in the United States of America

CONTENTS

TABLES AND GRAPHS

10   Contents

Expectations versus reality is something we all face. If our realities don't match our expectations, we're likely to be disappointed. Sometimes we feel cheated.

At times, we wish we'd had more accurate expectations. If we'd known what we were facing, perhaps we could have planned how to handle the realities a little better.

Adults tend to think teens' expectations are a world away from their realities. For some teens, this is probably an accurate view. For example, pregnant teens often appear unable to understand the realities ahead of them as they journey on to parenthood. One day, as I was teaching a parenting class of teen parents, my phone rang. The caller identified herself as a teen parent teacher in a school on the other side of Los Angeles. She then said vehemently, "How *do* you teach these kids reality?" And she waited for an answer!

I had no quick answer. "Teaching reality" is a hard assignment for several reasons. Teens tend to think "It can't happen to me" when they're confronted with a heavy dose of attempted reality indoctrination. And in all honesty, we *don't* know "it" will happen to any particular student.

Teens have a hard time facing reality because of their

developmental stage. Individuals in early adolescence simply are not ready to look far into the future. For some, thinking past Saturday night is difficult. So how can they be expected to face the hard realities of living with a partner, perhaps having a baby, and parenting that child?

Ten years ago I developed a questionnaire concerning teens' expectations of marriage. The questionnaire was administered to 3,118 teens, and the results were published in *Teens Look at Marriage: Rainbows, Roles and Reality* (1985: Morning Glory Press).

In 1993 I decided to find out how/if teens' perceptions/ expectations had changed during this decade. This time, however, I wanted to do a more thorough job of comparing teens' expectations with the realities of teens already living with a partner, so I developed two questionnaires. One was administered to 3,058 teens not yet married or living with a partner. The other was for teens already living with a partner—670 young men and women. Instead of responding to questions about their expectations of marriage or living together, they were asked to answer questions based on the realities they were experiencing in their partnership.

This book is a compilation of the project results. Responses of teens living with partners are compared with the expectations reported by the other group.

I learned quickly, as I had surmised, that the world of teenagers changed during the decade between 1984 and 1994, so I decided to include comparative data from the two surveys in *Teenage Couples—Expectations and Reality*.

The comparisons between the two time periods, and between teens already living with a partner and teens not yet together, provide valuable insight into the world of adolescents, insight that can help adults provide the relevant guidance teens need and want, guidance which will help them lead satisfying lives in the world of today.

Jeanne Warren Lindsay
January, 1996

The reality of the problems presented by teenage couples, parenting or not, compels us to take a hard objective look, to go beyond blame to trying to understand the situation better. Are our attempted and proposed solutions more compassionate and sane, on the one hand, or more ignorant and punitive on the other? Certainly many of them are inconsistent (make them stay home—put them in institutions), if not totally off the mark.

To know what will work, we need a deeper understanding of what is going on, and a more balanced point of view. *Teenage Couples—Expectations and Reality* gives us both: new insights into the situation gleaned from the protagonists, the teenage couples themselves, and a balance that encompasses concern for the babies, the teenage mothers, the fathers (whether teenage or older), the grandparents, the extended family, and the community.

Jeanne Warren Lindsay transcends narrow-mindedness and moralistic thinking as she plumbs the minds of teens about their attitudes, their expectations, and the realities of their lives. What better way to reach an understanding of these phenomena than to probe the hearts and thoughts of those who are most involved?

Her method of direct interviews, and her skill in communicating with the subjects, make this book readable as well as informative. It is a good balance of statistics, interviews, and commentary by the author. It is well researched, yet is practical and not too academic. The author has known for a long time that teens learn better from listening to other teens. And so can adults when the topic is teens!

Jeanne Lindsay says that twenty years ago when she started teaching teen parents, standard texts were not appropriate for students who already had babies. The books that were being used presented an impersonal approach to parenting that was not effective with real parents. This was the concern that inspired her to start her publishing house, Morning Glory Press.

Recognizing that materials for young people should be written in the second person in order to involve them, that the reading levels need to be suitable for their comprehension, and that they must be oriented to the present, Lindsay wrote such books. She identified gaps in the available literature: nothing about playing with one's child until she came along, nothing about the stress of three-generation living until she wrote a book with that title. The beginning of the recognition of the importance of the role of the father was heralded by Lindsay, and now she's done it again.

This time she's written a book that fills many gaps in our understanding. What is more, she suggests solutions to the dilemmas that face our nation in relation to teenage couples.

By shedding much light on these teenage couples and their *expectations* in relation to their *reality,* she's laid the groundwork for our working out more creative and humane solutions than have been suggested heretofore.

Lindsay speaks to the need for education for responsibility. Some of the conclusions drawn from her statistical analyses are startling. For example, that many young men, including some young fathers, don't plan or expect to work. Her interpretations of the results are revealing and should be read widely not only by educators and educational administrators but also by legislators, and more.

She compels us to look at the role of fathers free of former and current biases, and she notes the large percentage of dads who are older—not teenagers at all. This makes one pause and wonder why so much of the stigma falls on the mother. Why aren't some also seen as victims, girls used sexually by older men?

Myths and biases against young mothers returning to school are countered. She cites, for instance, that frequently very young women are more motivated toward going to school as a *result* of becoming mothers.

We should not be surprised that the author has done such a superb job because she approached the task from a rich background, not only in publishing, but also in studying anthropology, teaching pregnant teens, and writing teachers' guides to her eleven other outstanding books for parenting teens. But in addition to her education, professional experience and writing credits, Lindsay's intuitive powers and commitment—if not mission—to bring enlightenment to the problems of teenage couples illuminate this book.

Eugenie Wheeler, M.S.W.
Co-Author of ***Living Creatively with Chronic Illness: Developing Skills for Transcending the Loss, Pain and Frustration***

ACKNOWLEDGMENTS

I'm especially grateful to the 95 teachers and other professionals who administered the "Teen Expectations of and Realities in Marriage and Living Together" surveys to their students/clients and to those who referred young people to me for interviewing. I am even more grateful to the 3,728 young men and women who responded to the survey in 1994, and to the 80 young people who shared their lives so generously through the interviews they granted me. I learned a great deal from these young people and from the survey respondents.

Anita Mitchell, Sharon Enright, Sharon Rodine, Eugenie Wheeler, Judy Peterson, and Pati Lindsay read the manuscript at various stages of development, and contributed valuable suggestions and insight. I especially thank Eugenie Wheeler for the lovely Foreword.

Erin Lindsay prepared the graphs and tables, a formidable task, and Steve Lindsay contributed his expertise in the design of the book. David Crawford provided the lovely photos of teen couples from his classes at Daylor High School, Sacramento, California, and Tim Rinker designed the book's cover.

Carole Blum and Karen Blake helped with the proofreading and, perhaps more important, kept Morning Glory Press going during the considerable period of time I was wearing my book-writing blinders.

Bob, as always, was supportive throughout the long process of surveying, interviewing, writing, editing, proofreading, and all else that went into the production of this book.

To Bob
who understands the importance
of relationship-building,
and who continues to love me
as I love him.

"We don't want to get married, not for a long, long time."

3700 Teens Speak Out

I don't want to get married, not for a long, long time. I know we're together right now, we're tied down, but not all the way. Marriage seems like we would be stuck forever. I don't want to be like that.

He'd probably try to tell me everything I can't do. Then I'd feel bad if we split up, if we got divorced.

Angela, 16/Juan, 18 (Vaneza, 7 months)

Teenage Couples—Expectations and Reality

Far fewer teens marry today than in the past. Today, teenage couples are more likely to move in together without going through a marriage ceremony. Exact numbers are not available, however, for young couples living together without marriage. In fact, those numbers would be extremely hard to document because many teen couples live together only briefly.

What do teens expect of marriage? of living-together liaisons?

How do these expectations compare to the realities of teens already living with a partner? The study reported here was an attempt to find some answers directly from teenagers.

Decade of Change Documented

Teenage Couples—Expectations and Reality is based on two surveys, one in 1984 and the other in 1994, and on 80 extensive interviews (1994) with teens living with a partner. Results from the 1984 and 1994 surveys are compared. Responses from teens married or living with a partner (**Living-Together** or **L-T**) are compared with responses from those respondents who have never lived with a partner (**Single** or **S**). The survey was designed to obtain information concerning teens' expectations of marriage and other long-term relationships and of the realities of those already living with a partner.

For both surveys, volunteers, mostly family and consumer science and teen parent program teachers, agreed to administer the questionnaires to their students. Students were not paid for participating, nor were the professionals administering the questionnaires.

Respondents represented a variety of ethnic and religious groups, various areas of the United States, and rural and urban locations. Ages ranged from 12-20+, with 84 percent aged 15-18. See pages 22-24 for more details.

Make-Up of 1994 Study

For the 1994 study, two questionnaires were administered to a total of 3,728 young people, one to 3,058 teens not yet living with a partner, and the other to 670 teens who were living with a partner or had lived with a partner in the past. Two hundred of these "Living-Together" young people were no longer living with a partner, and they were asked to respond to the questionnaire according to the realities of that former relationship.

While the questionnaires were similar, the first focused on the respondents' expectations for their future marriage or living-together arrangements. For example, "How much do you think getting married or living with a partner at age 18 or younger

would change your life . . . ?" and "If/when you marry or live
with a partner, who should be responsible for preparing meals?"

The questionnaire for those already living with a partner
placed more emphasis on the realities of the respondents, as in
"How much has getting married or living with your partner
changed your life?" and "In *your* relationship, who is mostly
responsible for preparing meals?"

The complete Singles questionnaire is in the Appendix.
Questions 1-33 were the same for the Living-Together group, so
those questions are not repeated. Questions 34-120 and the nine
open-ended questions from the Living-Together survey are also
in the Appendix.

The survey included a mix of ethnic groups, rural and urban
youth, religious groups, and areas of the country. Females in the
Singles group outnumbered males three to one, while in the
Living-Together group, only 10.3 percent were males—601
females and 69 males. Ages ranged from 12 to over 20, with the
majority of those not living with a partner being 16 or 17. Of
those living together, the majority of females were 16 or 17, too,
while 72 percent of the males in this group were 17 or 18. See
pages 22-23 for more details.

The Singles group included 495 parenting teens; the Living-
Together group, 381. In the latter group, five out of eight of the
females and three out of four of the males had lived together less
than a year at the time they completed the survey. About half the
respondents said they started living with the partner before
pregnancy or parenthood occurred.

Nearly all respondents were in school, and the questionnaires
were administered by their teachers. Therefore, results do not
include information from young people who have dropped out
of school.

Nearly half of the Living-Together group were attending a
comprehensive high school or junior high. Almost as many were
attending a special school for pregnant and parenting teens or
another alternative school. Of the larger group (not living with a
partner), 12 percent were in a special school while nearly all the
others were in a comprehensive high school or junior high.

Single Survey Respondents — 1994

GENDER	Female	Male
Percentage	75.1	24.9
Number	2297	761

AGE	12-14		15		16		17		18+	
	F	M	F	M	F	M	F	M	F	M
Percentage	14.4	12.6	18.1	13.4	24.9	20.8	28.0	29.6	14.7	23.5
Number	329	96	415	102	570	158	641	225	336	178

SCHOOL GRADE	8 or Lower		9-10		11		12		Post High School	
	F	M	F	M	F	M	F	M	F	M
Percentage	20.8	18.0	46.3	40.5	29.6	37.5	3.0	3.2	.3	.9
Number	474	136	1060	307	678	285	69	24	8	7

KIND OF SCHOOL	High School or Junior High		Alternative Schools		"Other" School		Not in School	
	F	M	F	M	F	M	F	M
Percentage	84.6	93.0	14.3	5.6	.9	1.0	.3	.4
Number	1931	702	325	42	21	9	6	4

PLACE OF RESIDENCE	City		Suburb		Rural Area	
	F	M	F	M	F	M
Percentage	41.3	39.1	12.5	10.0	46.2	50.9
Number	940	294	284	75	1050	383

GEOGRAPHIC AREA	SE		NE		Midwest		SW		NW	
	F	M	F	M	F	M	F	M	F	M
Percentage	29.3	27.7	19.0	16.7	20.0	28.0	23.3	13.2	8.3	14.4
Number	672	210	438	127	460	213	536	100	191	109

ETHNICITY	White		Hispanic		Asian		Black		Native Amer.		Mixed	
	F	M	F	M	F	M	F	M	F	M	F	M
Percentage	42.0	47.5	11.9	10.4	.9	1.3	23.2	20.3	13.1	10.3	8.9	10.1
Number	946	356	268	78	21	10	524	152	295	77	201	76

RELIGION	Catholic		Protestant		Born-Again		Other		No Affiliation	
	F	M	F	M	F	M	F	M	F	M
Percentage	26.7	25.4	13.5	12.1	15.9	16.4	27.0	28.0	16.8	18.1
Number	605	191	307	91	361	123	613	211	382	136

MARITAL STATUS	Single		Engaged		Married		Separated		Divorced/ Widowed	
	F	M	F	M	F	M	F	M	F	M
Percentage	87.2	91.2	10.6	4.9	.6	.8	1.2	1.2	.5	1.9
Number	1992	689	242	37	13	6	27	9	12	14

HAS CHILD	No		One		Two		Three		4 or More	
	F	M	F	M	F	M	F	M	F	M
Percentage	80.7	91.1	17.5	5.0	1.3	.8	.3	.8	.2	2.3
Number	1795	662	389	36	29	6	7	6	5	17

Living-Together Survey Respondents — 1994

GENDER	Female	Male
Percentage	89.7	10.3
Number	601	69

AGE	13-14		15-16		17		18		19+	
	F	M	F	M	F	M	F	M	F	M
Percentage	1.9	0.0	26.9	11.6	35.1	30.4	24.6	42.0	11.5	15.9
Number	11	0	162	8	211	21	148	29	69	11

SCHOOL GRADE	8 or Lower		9-10		11		12		Post High School	
	F	M	F	M	F	M	F	M	F	M
Percentage	8.0	10.1	41.2	26.1	43.5	52.2	6.4	11.6	1.0	0.0
Number	48	7	246	18	260	36	38	8	6	0

KIND OF SCHOOL	High School or Junior High		Alternative Schools		"Other" School		Not in School	
	F	M	F	M	F	M	F	M
Percentage	46.1	68.1	47.9	23.1	4.6	1.4	1.4	7.2
Number	268	47	278	16	27	1	8	5

PLACE OF RESIDENCE	City		Suburb		Rural Area	
	F	M	F	M	F	M
Percentage	61.3	60.9	15.6	13.0	23.0	26.1
Number	365	42	93	9	137	18

GEOGRAPHIC AREA	SE		NE		Midwest		SW		NW	
	F	M	F	M	F	M	F	M	F	M
Percentage	11.5	5.8	11.5	15.9	14.0	29.0	48.3	21.7	14.8	27.5
Number	69	4	69	11	84	20	290	15	89	19

ETHNICITY	White		Hispanic		Asian		Black		Native Amer.		Mixed	
	F	M	F	M	F	M	F	M	F	M	F	M
Percentage	33.4	46.9	34.3	17.2	1.9	3.1	10.7	12.5	10.7	6.3	9.0	14.1
Number	197	30	202	11	11	2	63	8	63	4	53	9

RELIGION	Catholic		Protestant		Born-Again		Other		No Affiliation	
	F	M	F	M	F	M	F	M	F	M
Percentage	34.6	19.1	7.6	2.9	13.5	16.2	20.1	29.4	24.3	32.4
Number	205	13	45	2	80	11	119	20	144	22

MARITAL STATUS	Single		Engaged		Married		Separated		Divorced/ Widowed	
	F	M	F	M	F	M	F	M	F	M
Percentage	61.9	78.3	15.0	13.0	18.0	5.8	4.3	2.9	.8	0.0
Number	364	54	88	9	106	4	25	2	5	0

HAS CHILD	No		One		Two		Three		4 or More	
	F	M	F	M	F	M	F	M	F	M
Percentage	40.7	52.9	50.8	36.8	7.1	5.9	1.2	4.4	.2	0.0
Number	240	36	299	25	42	4	7	3	1	0

All Survey Respondents — 1984

GENDER	Female	Male
Percentage	77.3	22.7
Number	2410	708

AGE	14 or younger		15		16		17		18+	
	F	M	F	M	F	M	F	M	F	M
Percentage	6.3	3.9	35.4	33.4	28.2	28.6	26.2	30.0	3.9	4.1
Number	218	43	354	91	589	168	707	198	487	190

SCHOOL GRADE	8 or Lower		9-10		11		12		Not in School	
	F	M	F	M	F	M	F	M	F	M
Percentage	6.3	3.9	35.3	33.4	28.2	28.6	26.2	30.0	3.9	4.1
Number	146	27	827	229	659	196	611	206	92	28

PLACE OF RESIDENCE	Inner City		Urban Area		Suburb		Town 10,000 or Less		Farm	
	F	M	F	M	F	M	F	M	F	M
Percentage	29.8	20.8	22.9	17.6	20.2	34.4	17.4	14.6	9.8	12.5
Number	694	143	532	121	469	236	405	100	227	86

GEOGRAPHIC AREA	SE		NE		Midwest		SW		NW	
	F	M	F	M	F	M	F	M	F	M
Percentage	10.6	7.6	10.2	10.2	22.2	23.2	44.0	52.4	13.2	6.7
Number	250	57	241	76	525	173	1043	391	312	50

ETHNIC GROUP	Black		White		Asian		Native Amer.		Hispanic	
	F	M	F	M	F	M	F	M	F	M
Percentage	17.9	8.7	58.2	60.6	1.3	2.2	5.0	7.2	17.5	21.3
Number	417	59	1355	413	31	15	116	49	408	145

RELIGION	Catholic		Born-Again		Protestant		Jewish		Other	
	F	M	F	M	F	M	F	M	F	M
Percentage	41.0	48.3	18.9	19.5	14.7	13.9	.8	.7	24.6	17.7
Number	859	292	396	118	307	84	17	4	515	107

MARITAL STATUS	Single		Engaged		Married		Separated		Divorced/ Widowed	
	F	M	F	M	F	M	F	M	F	M
Percentage	80.7	90.2	12.1	6.0	6.3	2.3	.7	1.0	.2	.1
Number	1898	618	284	41	147	16	17	7	5	3

Of the Living-Together females, almost 99 percent were still in school, a far higher percentage than that of the general population of school-age wives/partners and mothers. Conclusions drawn from statistics based on responses from this group should include consideration of this pro-school bias, and of the bias toward alternative schools, especially those for pregnant and parenting teens.

Students from forty-nine states responded to the Singles questionnaire. (Results from an Idaho school were lost en route.) Forty-three states were represented by the Living-Together sample. See pages 22-23 for regional breakdown of participants.

All questionnaires were completed anonymously. Answer sheets together with any additional comments from respondents were returned to me by mail. The resulting data were coded by Survey and Ballot Systems, Inc., Eden Prairie, Minnesota using the SPSS statistical software program.

Earlier Study Described

In 1984 I designed and organized the administration of a similar questionnaire to 3,118 young people. This group included 359 teens who were married and/or living with a partner. Only one questionnaire was used, but an additional section was included for the Living-Together group.

As in the more recent study, teachers, mostly in home economics classes and teen parent programs, volunteered to administer the questionnaire to their students. The resulting data were analyzed by Nick Konnoff using the SPSS program. As in 1994, various ethnic groups, religious faiths, and areas of the country were represented. See page 24 for details.

Age breakdown was similar to the 1994 group. Males were slightly less well-represented, making up 22.7 percent of the total group. About two-fifths of the female respondents had been pregnant, and three percent had had abortions. About 20 percent of the young men either said they had caused a pregnancy or didn't know. Of the 379 mothers in the survey, less than half (180) had babies older than six months. Only 34 had children aged two years or older.

For some of the questions, responses from the 1994 survey were quite different from those of a decade earlier. Most of the following chapters include some comparisons between young people's responses in 1984 and 1994.

Obviously, not all of the survey data could be included in *Teenage Couples—Expectations and Reality.* This report focuses on changes during the decade between 1984 and 1994, and on differences between the expectations of Single respondents and the realities of Living-Together teens. When respondents from the earlier survey are not included, it is generally because responses differed little from those provided by teens in 1994, or, in a few cases, because comparative data is not available from the earlier study.

In the narrative I have attempted to strike a balance between providing study data and making the book quickly readable for those who want only the basic information. Bar and circle graphs are frequently used to illustrate specific points. More detailed back-up data are available on request from Morning Glory Press.

Interviews Offer Additional Insight

As an anthropologist, however, I don't believe that statistics are enough. Some hopes, dreams, and realities can be counted, but many cannot. The people behind these statistics are real teenagers, each one different from all the others.

In order to learn more about teenagers as individuals, in 1994 I interviewed 80 young people already living with a partner. The basic questions I asked these young people were similar, but when an individual appeared especially interested or competent in a particular topic, I often focused on that topic as we talked.

I recorded most of the interviewees' comments verbatim in shorthand, and transcribed each interview. Quotes are taken directly from these interviews, although some of the quotes are a compilation of an individual's responses to various questions.

I was continually amazed at the openness these young people exhibited as they talked about their problems and their joys, and the wisdom which many shared during these interviews.

Interview Data — 1994

GENDER	Male			Female			
	26			54			

AGE	14	15	16	17	18	19	20	21+
	1	3	11	19	19	8	7	12

Note: All were living with a partner before age 20 or, if older, lived with a partner younger than 20.

LIVED TOGETHER	1 yr.	1-2 yr.	2-3 yr.	3+ yr.
	25	36	12	7

MARRIED?	Yes		No	
	31		49	

ETHNICITY	Hispanic	White	Black	Native Am.	Asian
	28	30	12	7	3

NUMBER OF	None	Pregnant	1	2	3
CHILDREN	4	7	58	10	1

Description of Interviewees

Thirty-one of the interviewees were married, and for 13 couples, both husband and wife were interviewed.

Of the 31 married interviewees, 18 did not live together before they were married while 13 did.

Twelve of the interviewees were no longer living with their partner, although three were still "together."

Sixty-five of the 80 interviewees had lived with a partner at his or her parents' home. Half of the total group were still with parents at the time of the interview, while 40 were living by themselves at that time.

Almost half of the interviewees (39) were living in California. Other states represented included Florida, Georgia, Nebraska, Ohio, Pennsylvania, Illinois, Montana, and Oregon.

Comments of the young people interviewed were used extensively in the two books written and published especially for teens, *Teenage Couples—Caring, Commitment and Change* and *Teenage Couples—Coping with Reality* (1995: Morning Glory

Press), with the belief that other teenagers would learn more from these young people than from anything a professional could say. Additional comments are used in *Teenage Couples— Expectations and Reality,* but for a different reason. Adults who work with teenagers need to be acutely aware of the culture of school-age couples, a culture which includes many school-age parents. I believe these young people's comments give insight into this special culture, a culture quite different from that of couples a few years older.

While quotes are from the same group of individuals quoted in the other two *Teenage Couples* books, the comments used here, with only two or three exceptions, are different from those in the other books. Quotes with names are from interviews. Quotes without names are taken from individuals' written reponses to the open-ended questions in the survey.

Interviews in an Earlier Time — 1984

Quotes in this book are entirely from the 1994 interviews and survey. The 1984 study included 76 interviews, but no attempt was made to compare quotes of the two periods.

Comparisons of the make-up of the two groups, however, provides further insight into changes among teenage couples during this decade. Of the 76 young people interviewed in 1984, 60 females and 16 males, 65 were or had been married, as compared to 31 in the 1994 group.

Four interviewees were single mothers who had not lived with a partner. Only seven Living-Together couples were represented in the 1984 group, and all of the male interviewees were married.

In both 1984 and 1994, the intent of the project was to interview teen couples, whether married or living together. I didn't focus only on married couples in 1984 nor did I ignore married informants in 1994. My criteria were teen couples who were living with a partner at the time of the interview or had done so at an earlier time. Whether they were married or not was not a factor in their selection. The interview group comparison is another indication of the change in the culture of teenage couples, the trend away from marriage and toward living together.

Project Summary

Teenage Couples—Expectations and Reality is based on:

- 1994 survey of 3,058 Single teens' expectations of marriage and living together.
- 1994 survey of 670 Living-Together teens' views on the realities in their relationships.
- 1984 survey of 3,118 teens' expectations of marriage and living together.
- Additional analyses of the 359 married/living-together teens included in the 1984 survey.
- Eighty interviews of teens living with a partner, interviews conducted in 1994.

Teenage Couples—Expectations and Reality is not meant to replace either *Teenage Couples—Caring, Commitment and Change* or *Teenage Couples—Coping with Reality.* These two books were written specifically for teenagers wishing to learn how to work on building a good relationship with a partner. Each offers many suggestions for achieving that goal.

Teenage Couples—Expectations and Reality is designed to be used as background material for teachers using the other two books in this series in a relationship or other class. It could be utilized as a supplementary text in a sociology class and/or as resource material for research papers. It is especially meant for anyone, of whatever age, who is interested in how teens are thinking today.

This book contains a great deal of information about teenage relationships and teenagers' attitudes toward those relationships, but it doesn't offer a lot of advice. It is meant to provide insight into the culture of teenage couples, thereby helping teachers, other professionals, students and parents increase their understanding of teenagers' attitudes toward marriage and living together and to learn of the realities of teenage partnerships.

*"Neither of us is really ready to be tied down forever.
We're too young and we're not ready financially."*

CHAPTER 1

Searching for Love — But Not for Marriage

We're too young and we're not ready financially. I think when you're married, you're tied down, you have more of a commitment. But living together is just like being with your girlfriend.

Meghan, 18/Justin, 21 (Jameka, 2½ years)

Neither of us is really ready to be tied down forever. I'm not one for wanting to get married. I don't want to get married because of my pregnancy.

I preferred living together instead of getting married. Marriage is a very big commitment and I didn't want that. He's older than me, and we're still not ready.

Summer, 15/Daesun, 20 (Cecelia, 9 months)

Don't rush anything, and if you stay together, ain't no need to get married.

Male respondent, 17

Most Teens Don't Marry

A century ago, the median age of first marriage in the United States was 16. Ten years ago, that age had jumped to 23. Today, it's even higher—26.5 for males and 24.5 for females.[1]

In 1950, 17.1 percent of women and 3.3 percent of men married before they were 20. By 1980 that percentage had fallen to 8 percent of the females and 2 percent of the males.[2]

Even fewer teenagers marry today. Only one percent of men and 4.1 percent of women aged 15-19 are married[3] (figure 1.1).

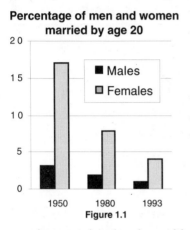

Percentage of men and women married by age 20

Males

Females

1950   1980   1993

Figure 1.1

Pregnancy, a big reason for early marriage in other times, is no longer considered a valid motive. Today, only 29 percent of the teenage mothers in the United States are married when they give birth, a fact which dismays many adults because children are more at risk for health, social, and economic problems if they are raised by a single parent. Teens, however, are more likely to believe marriage won't solve the problems.

In the majority of teenage pregnancies in the United States, the father of the baby is an adult man. In fact, nine out of ten births to all single mothers in this country involve fathers over 20. Adult men father 71 percent of the births among school-age girls, according to researcher Mike Males.[4] These facts bring up other important questions, but this project, a study of teenage relationships, did not deal with those questions.

The project did study teens' attitudes concerning sex before

[1]Census Bureau, Current Population Survey, Marital Status and Living Arrangements, March, 1993.

[2]*Teenage Pregnancy: The Problem That Hasn't Gone Away* (1981: The Alan Guttmacher Institute).

[3] Census Bureau, March, 1993.

[4] *PSAY Network,* June, 1995.

marriage, living together without marriage, marriage because of pregnancy, and the man's responsibility in a pregnancy. Teens' attitudes on these topics have changed since 1984.

Sex Before Marriage

Most of the survey respondents were 18 or younger. According to *Sex and America's Teenagers* (1994: Allan Guttmacher Institute), 64 percent of males and 52 percent of females in the United States have had sexual intercourse by age 18.

In both surveys, teens were asked if they thought it was all right for couples to have intercourse before they marry. As might be expected, more teens today approve of sex before marriage as compared with teens in the 1984 study (figure 1.2).

Although only a minority thought having sexual intercourse before marriage was wrong, several respondents commented on their negative feelings on this issue:

> *It's not a good idea, especially since I'm Catholic, but I did have sex with my boyfriend because my morals didn't go through my head when I was doing that. Besides, I love him a lot, so it's hard to say. But if you don't love the person, it's not a good idea.*

Female respondent, 15

Is sex before marriage okay?

Combined responses: *"Absolutely," "Probably,"* and *"It doesn't matter."*

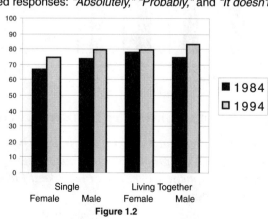

Figure 1.2

Looking back on her own life, another informant, 17, was even more opposed to early sex:

> *Actually, I think it (sex before marriage) is wrong, but I was brought out of my virgin stage during my ninth grade year. If I could take it back, I would, and wait until I get married, but I also got pregnant. So I would say, absolutely not, because you miss out on a lot of things once you've made that big step.*
>
> Female respondent, 17

Teens today, as compared to 1984 teens, are more accepting of a couple living together before they marry. In 1994, more than four in five of the Single respondents and nine in ten of the Living-Togethers said either "Okay" or "It's okay *if* they plan to marry later" (figure 1.3).

Okay to live together without marriage?

Combined responses: *"Okay"* and *"Okay If they plan to marry later."*

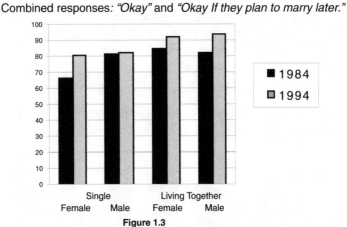

Figure 1.3

Some find that moving in with a partner doesn't work:

> *I wish I had stayed at home. I regret it, but what is done is done. With all these problems here, I sometimes think it would be best for me to leave. Then I feel like if I leave, I'll never see him again.*
>
> Trina, 16/Victor, 16 (Felipe, 3 months)

Others offered advice:

If you want to move in with somebody, you have to give it your all. When you move in, you can't do it half-way. If you don't think you're going to make it, don't try it.

Heather, 15/Brandon, 20 (Alexis, 13 months)

Marrying Because of Pregnancy

With a big majority of all the groups believing sex before marriage is acceptable, and it's all right to live together before marriage, it's no surprise that many of these young people already are pregnant or have a child.

We asked how they feel about marrying because of pregnancy, a "solution" in the past to unplanned pregnancy. Very few felt teenagers should marry because of pregnancy, far fewer than in 1984 (figure 1.4).

When a teenage couple gets pregnant, should they get married?
Combined responses: *"Absolutely"* and *"Probably"*

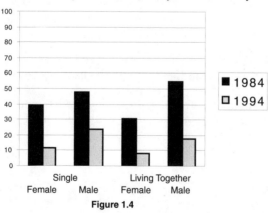

Figure 1.4

Respondents in all groups were overwhelmingly positive, however, about the man sharing responsibility for any pregnancy he causes and for his child (figure 1.5).

A large majority, about eight in ten of all the Singles and the Living-Together females and nine in ten of the Living-Together males, think it's important for a child to live with both of his/her parents. However, among the responding 381 Living-Together *parents,* only 211 lived with their child's other parent, and only one in five of the Living-Together group were actually married (figure 1.6).

If a man gets a woman pregnant, should he take responsibility for the pregnancy and the child? *"Absolutely"* or *"Probably"*

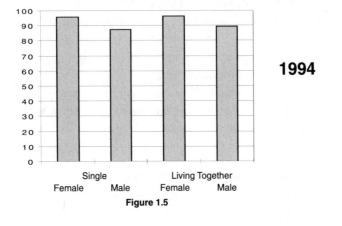

Figure 1.5

Percentage of all respondents who believe it is "absolutely" or "probably" important for a child to live with both parents and
Percentage of 381 Living-Together *Parent* Respondents who are married to child's other parent

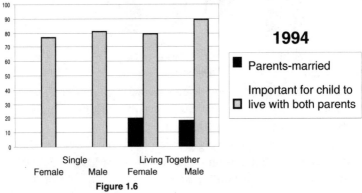

Figure 1.6

Realistically, a man is generally more likely to be "responsible" for his child if he lives with *and* is married to the child's mother. There are, of course, exceptions. See chapter 10 for data concerning teenage fathers' involvement with their children. Three-fourths of the Single fathers report involvement with their child, and most of the Living-Together fathers either live with their children or see them at least occasionally. Some of the fathers not living with their children see them daily.

Optimistic as these figures are, they leave many children *not* involved with their fathers, a fact not in line with the values the respondents expressed in this study.

Reasons to Marry

Troy and Sandra were among those who decided to marry. He explained:

> *If we just lived together, I could go off when I wanted, but when you're married, your first responsibility is to your wife. Instead of going out with your friends, you're with her.*
>
> *With a four-month-old baby, there are more changes than ever. But we didn't worry about the changes. We were ready, at least I was. I've been around kids a lot so I thought I knew what it would take.*
>
> *It's kind of different, though, when the baby's yours— you can't just give it to your girlfriend!*
>
> Troy, 21/Sandra, 18 (Violet, 16 weeks)

Respondents who were married were asked, "Why did you decide on marriage rather than living together?" Of the thirty-three responding, ten said living together was wrong without marriage. Four others married because of their religious beliefs.

> *I didn't think we should just live together. We would have begun sinning with sex. We were in love. We prayed about it, we weighed the pros and cons of each, and marriage was the best idea.*
>
> Female respondent, 16

One respondent said, "Because I had to," and four had parents who would not approve of the young couple living together without marriage. The other 14 said either "We're both ready for marriage" or "We were planning to marry anyway."

> *Derek and I love each other very much and we couldn't wait to be together. Both of us grew up believing it's wrong to live together without being married. It's not wrong to live together, but it is wrong to have sex if you aren't married.*
>
> Female respondent, 17

Living Together Versus Marriage

The fact is, however, that not many teens, whether parents or not, are getting married these days. For some, marriage means long-term commitment, and they are not ready for that. But that does not mean, in their minds, that they aren't "ready" to live together.

Many teens in this survey are living with a partner. Only 18 percent of the females and 6 percent of the males are married to that partner, although a majority of those living together are pregnant or already have children. (The slightly higher percentage shown as married on page 36 refers only to those respondents who are parents. The above percentage is based on information from all Living-Together respondents.)

Why is the overwhelming majority of this sample not married? Meghan offered a typical response:

> *We talked about it a lot, but there were more important things we needed to do first before we got married, like graduate from high school, grow up a little bit. We talked about it and how we needed to grow up before we got married.*
>
> *We agreed that if we wanted to get married, we wanted to go into it thinking this is forever. We both wanted it to be forever, and you can't guarantee that when you're still changing.*
>
> *We were together when we were so young. I was 13 and*

he was 16. I had dated a little bit, but nothing like when I went with him.

Meghan, 18/Justin, 21 (Jameka, 21/2 years)

At one time, a pregnant teen who didn't marry was assumed to be a teen whose partner refused to marry her. A "wronged woman," she was called. Conventional wisdom suggested that of course the woman would be married if the man was willing.

According to this survey, that conventional wisdom no longer represents teens. Of the 362 Living-Together teens who completed the open-ended questions, 166, most of them female, explained why they weren't married. Only one said, "He doesn't want to (get married)."

Most, 125, said they were too young, not ready, or decided to wait to see if they were compatible.

Anita and Jarrod have been living together for seven months. Anita explained why they have not yet married:

We didn't get married because there are a lot of problems with getting married. It changes a lot, and we like the way we are right now. We want to let our love grow.

Sometimes when people marry when they're too young, they grow apart. We want our relationship to keep growing.

Anita, 18/Jarrod, 25 (Jarrod, Jr., 4 months)

In nine cases, the parents refused to sign the papers permitting the marriage. Eighteen respondents said they didn't have enough money to get married. Eight simply "didn't want to get married." Others replied, "Because I knew it wouldn't work out," "because he's 38 and I'm 17," "I don't want to be tied down for the rest of my life," and "Marriage is so permanent!"

The Moral Issue

Unlike a generation ago, many of these young couples appear to believe strongly that it would not be *right* to marry too soon—even though they have decided to live together. Most see marriage as being permanent, and they aren't ready for that.

Maurice, like many teens in the survey and others who were interviewed, is determined that when he does marry, there will be no break-up:

> *Marriage? I don't know. To me personally, marriage is not really an option right now. I plan on getting married one day. If I do get married, it will be to Mitzuko. There are so many people who want us to get married. They say you might as well, you're the same as married.*
>
> *But to me, marriage means something you can never go back on. I'm a firm believer in no divorce, no separation. Once you get married, you have to take anything, anything.*
>
> *When my parents separated, I promised myself I would never never ever get married until I really felt it was the time. People say, "Oh, you'd be such a cute couple, and you'd have such a nice wedding."*
>
> *We're a cute couple now. And I don't think a baby is a reason to get married. If we didn't have a baby, there would be no talk of marriage.*

Maurice, 20/Mitzuko, 16 (Lana, 14 months)

Is sex an important part of your relationship?

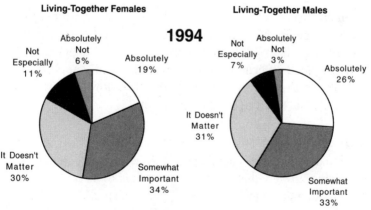

Figure 1.7

Importance of Sex

About nine out of ten of the Single teens thought sex would be an important part of marriage or a living-together relationship.

Sex, however, is "absolutely not" or "probably not" important or "It doesn't matter" to almost half the women and two of five men (figure 1.7).

Erin Kathleen, happily married for two years to Joe, explained:

> *Some kids think it must be great to be married because they think the sex lasts all the time. You don't have to hide it from your parents anymore. They say, "You must have such an exciting time together."*
>
> *They think the sex is going to be exciting and romantic, but when you get married, it isn't really like that. They think the excitement will last forever. Then when you get married, it doesn't, and you think maybe you don't love him any more. "Maybe we don't really love each other. Everything was so much more exciting and new, and we just thought we were in love." You have to get over how things used to be and build new things.*

Erin Kathleen, 18/Joe, 21

Summary and Conclusions

The values expressed by a majority of these young people suggest:

It's all right to have sex before marriage.

It's okay for a man and woman to live together without being married.

A teenage couple should not marry because of pregnancy.

The father should take responsibility for the pregnancy and for his child.

It is important for a child to live with both parents.

Marriage is forever and divorce is bad, so it's better simply to live together rather than marry.

The real problem, I believe, is not that teen parents don't marry. The problem is the fact of too-early-parenthood which often causes problems for mothers, fathers, babies, extended families, and for society. But these problems are not likely to go away if the young parents simply get married.

Parents who are not married can parent together. Parents who don't live together can share parenting, even parents who don't like each other, but parenting under such arrangements tends to produce a difficult scenario for the individuals involved.

Many of these young people feel strongly that marriage is a life-long commitment. In their view, marriage "should" be postponed until one is absolutely ready for that commitment. By itself, this view is a strong statement on the value of families staying together "forever," and of the importance to children of their parents remaining together.

Over and over young fathers have said to me, "My father wasn't around when I was growing up. I don't want that for my child." About nine in ten of these young people feel the father should be responsible for his child. Almost as many feel a child should live with both parents. Both are strong family values.

At the same time, young people appear to accept living with a partner before marriage as an acceptable value.

The sad reality is that the break-up of a couple can be devastating even if they are not married and therefore do not divorce. If the couple has a child, then split up, the child is likely to be hurt as much as if his parents went through a divorce.

Two hundred of the 670 Living-Together respondents no longer were living with a partner when they completed the questionnaire. The Living-Together arrangement did not work out for them.

Johnny Angel speaks to this topic on page 22 of *Teenage Couples—Caring, Commitment and Change:*

> *I feel if a relationship is serious enough to have intimacy, it should also be serious enough to think ahead. Frankly, if the individual is not somebody you want to be with in the future, you shouldn't make a bond by having a child.*

A lot of times the younger teens think it's all fun and games. It's not when you have another little life at stake. She is the casualty of the fun and games, especially if the other parent is somebody you really don't care about and you don't want to stay together. What's to happen to that child?

Johnny Angel, 19/Davina, 19 (Valizette, 11 days)

Young people need to consider a lot of questions before moving in together—*and before getting pregnant.* Is either parent earning enough money to support the family? Do either or both parents need to be in school rather than home caring for the baby or out earning a living? What about their emotional readiness for marriage? For parenthood?

We used to call teen love "puppy love," suggesting that it wasn't a serious thing. We realize now that teen love can be very powerful. Add the sexually explicit, sexually stimulating world of today, and it's not surprising that so many teens are getting pregnant and moving in with their partners before they are ready to develop a long-lasting, caring relationship with each other.

As adults, our role is to help teens cope with the realities of their world as it is today, rather than with a culture which supports early marriage, a culture which no longer exists for many of our young people.

As teachers, counselors, parents, and others who care about young people, we have a responsibility to encourage them to delay parenting until both parents are ready. We need to accept the realities of teens' values, values which, for many, do not include delaying sex until marriage. We need to work much harder at helping teens become responsible, whether "being responsible" means delaying sexual intercourse or protecting themselves from too-early pregnancy. We especially need to help teens develop the skills that lead to successful, "forever" relationships *when they're ready.*

*"A teenager's dream is to move out on their own,
party all the time—but it's the impossible dream."*

CHAPTER **2**

Change Happens —
Can We Cope?

*We always had fun at the parks and things like that.
When we weren't fighting, we got along great. We were like
two little puppies laughing and playing.*

*Our partnership has not lasted. In fact, she hates me
and she's blaming me for us breaking up. Now she won't
let me see our son, so I'm going to take her to court and
fight for Jose's custody.*

Male respondent, 16

Here is a bitter young man. Things changed in his life. He
remembers good times in his relationship with his girlfriend, but
those times are gone. They have a son, but this young man feels
he won't be allowed to parent his child unless he fights for
custody in court. Changes do, indeed, happen.

Joe and Erin Kathleen, after two years of marriage,
pondered the changes in their lives:

We both realize now that maybe we should have waited until we were older to get married because there's a lot of stuff we've missed. We almost split up over that, stuff I missed, a lot of things we can't get back.

When I turned 21 I could go to bars, but when you're married, it's not right. Her mom called me all kinds of stuff for hanging out in a bar. Erin Kathleen missed a lot of dances at school. She missed a lot more than I did. We went to the prom but it wasn't really the same.

Joe, 21/Erin Kathleen, 18

All his friends were changing, moving out, turning 21, going out to party with no strings attached. Joe was kind of jealous because they got to do a lot of things he'd like to do. I think that was hard for him. They used to be his good friends in high school, and they grew apart. They'd think, "Joe and Erin Kathleen are married, and she wouldn't let him go out all hours of the night." And I do kind of think that way, and Joe knows that.

Actually we split up for a couple of weeks. We were miserable, and then we talked, and we don't know why we split. Things are going well now.

Erin Kathleen

Has S/he Changed?

It was weird, living together. Joshua changed a lot from what he was when we weren't living together. We fought, he wouldn't work, he was a different person. When he turned 18, he could go to the bars. He'd always go out and I'd stay home. All he thought about was going out.

Arkameia, 18/Joshua, 20 (Erica, 13 months)

One-quarter of the women and almost one-third of the men reported either some or much negative change in their partners after they started living together. Responses from females had not changed appreciably since 1984, but nearly twice as many males in 1994 saw negative changes in their partners after they started living together (figure 2.1).

**Has your partner changed
since you started living together?**
"Some" or *"Much negative change"*

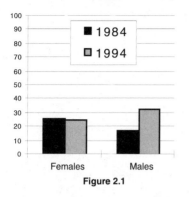

Figure 2.1

Many of the young people we interviewed spoke of changes in their life plans because of their early partnership:

> *It's a lot harder to live together. You think it will be all nice—he'll do this, you'll do that, you'll be a cute little couple. Then you find how people really are. They have fights with their siblings. It's a whole new story when you're living with somebody. It's like a whole different culture even if it's the same background. It's different, and if you don't take it like that, you'll have a much harder time adjusting.*
>
> *If you have a child, that makes it that much more difficult. You'll each have your own ideas of how to raise your child.*
>
> Mitzuko, 16/Maurice, 20 (Lana, 14 months)

Women in 1994 were more likely than those in 1984 to find living together harder than they had expected. The opposite was true of male respondents (figure 2.2).

"Living together is harder than I expected."

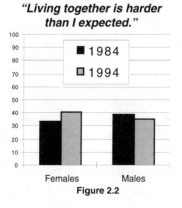

Figure 2.2

> *When Daesun first moved in, it was pretty good, but it's changed a lot. Being around somebody constantly every day, it's like you get tired and frustrated with that person. Then you start to argue, and you get fed up.*

We argue constantly. Sometimes we walk away from it,
but most of the time I drag things on and try to make him
tell me anything that might help.
   We fight basically over stupid stuff. We fight over the
baby. If I want to go somewhere or he wants to go
somewhere, we argue about that.

                                    Summer, 15/Daesun, 20 (Cecelia, 9 months)

Changes — Expected and Real

Respondents not yet living with a partner were asked about
changes they might expect if they married or moved in with a
partner before reaching 18. Questions for the Living-Together
group asked about changes they experienced after moving
in with a partner. (Thirty percent of the Living-Together
respondents were no longer living with their partners.)

Questions dealt with changes, expected and real, such as
friends (fewer or more?), recreation, and free time (time for
oneself). According to the responses, realities for the males were
quite different from those of the females.

Fewer Friends

When we first met, I had friends. I left them, but he
hasn't left his. He likes hanging out with his friends a
whole lot.
   Now that we're married, I tell him he should stay away
from them because they're a bad influence. He likes to
party and I don't, but I think he's changing.

                                    Celina, 17/Scott, 20 (Melanie, 6 weeks)

Only 23 percent of the Single respondents expected to have
fewer friends after marriage or moving in with a partner. Realities of the Living-Together group showed half again as many of
the Living-Together *women* having fewer friends now than
before the move-in. For the young men, however, moving in
with a partner changed their friendship pattern only to the degree
forecast by the Single males (figure 2.3).

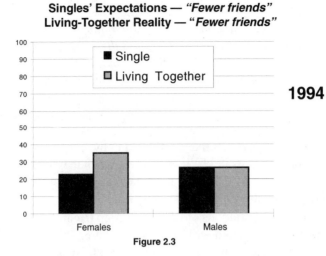

Singles' Expectations — *"Fewer friends"*
Living-Together Reality — *"Fewer friends"*

Figure 2.3

Through an open-ended question, Living-Together respondents were asked, "What do you feel you have given up because of your partnership?" The answer most often was "Friends." Of the 362 teens responding to the open-ended questions, ninety-nine gave this answer. Nineteen young women listed "His friends" as "the biggest problem in our partnership." In addition, 37 listed friends as the subject of many of their arguments.

> *Sam's friends come around a lot. We get along with them, but they know we don't want them here all the time. When Sam used to leave with them, I said, "How would you like it if I did that?"*
>
> *He said he wouldn't like it. I said, "That's what you need to think about when you make your decisions. How would Myra like it?" We always have to think about the other person.*
>
> *He did, and he told his friends that if he wants to be with them, he will go looking for them. A friend called the other day and asked him to go out. Sam said, "No, my baby is coming and I want to be with Myra."*
>
> Myra, 17/Sam, 18

Changes in Recreation

A teenager's dream is to move out on their own, party all the time, stay out all night, do all these things. I find that Zaid is still like that sometimes, but it's the impossible dream. We have to be home to put the baby to bed, and I'm exhausted by that time.

Tameka, 17/Zaid, 22 (Chantilly, 6 months)

As for partying, half the young men in the expectations survey said there would be less partying when they married or moved in with a partner. Men living with a partner, however, found their realities included slightly *more* partying than indicated by the expectations of the other group (figure 2.4).

For women, again it was a different picture. The majority of the young women found their partying decidedly decreasing after moving in with a partner (figure 2.4).

There's more tears involved in being
a teenager and married than my friends think.

Singles' Expectations —
"Less recreation/partying when/if I move in with partner."

Living-Together Reality —
"Less recreation/partying since I moved in with partner."

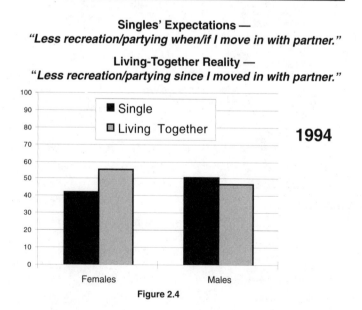

Figure 2.4

There's more tears involved in being a teenager and married than my friends think. They will ask me to go to somebody's party, and someone else will say, "She can't, she's married," and that sucks. I was pretty popular in middle school, and then I didn't go to high school at all my first year because I was on Independent Study because I was pregnant.

I had about 15 friends who would call me on a regular basis. Now I have only about four who call me.

Jillian, 17/Richard, 18 (Kevin, 15 months)

The two groups' expectations of more, less, or no change in free time available after moving in with a partner varied little. The realities were as expected — less free time for nearly two-thirds of the respondents.

Risk of Too-Early Relationship

An individual who marries or moves in with a partner while still a teenager frequently has not had time to develop a firm individual identity. S/he has not experienced a typical adolescence, and after awhile may fantasize about the "single carefree life" s/he has missed.

> *I wanted to move in with him so I could be free.*

Eighteen of the Living-Together group who responded to the open-ended questions said because of their partnership, they had given up their childhood or their teenage years. Eight others said they missed "freedom to flirt, date other people." Seventy-seven of these young people reported giving up their freedom, and four replied that they had given up "everything."

Several survey respondents and interviewees discussed their feelings after settling down with one partner in their mid-teens:

I wanted to move in with him so I could be free, and we are a lot happier now that we don't have to worry about

*my mom telling me what time to be home. I want to wait
until I finish school to get married.*

*I hope it will last forever, but I've been with him since I
was 15, and now I'm almost 19 and more guys have
started asking me out lately. Sometimes I want to, but I
don't because I love my fiance and I want us to stay
together.*

Female respondent, 18

*Me and Angela are together, but I still find my eyes
wandering. Sometimes I think, "I'm just 18, why ain't I out
there?" One of the big problems about having a relationship so young is you tend to regret it. You know you have to
mature so quick.*

Juan, 18/Angela, 16 (Vaneza, 7 months)

Teens change rapidly as they develop. In addition, living
together, whether married or not, changes people. Teen couples
often find they must adjust to more changes than they expected.

Summary and Conclusions

Teens already living with a partner found more changes in
their lives than were anticipated by the Single teens. Women,
especially, found they had fewer friends and were less free to go
out after moving in with partners. Teen men, however, tended to
have about as many friends and to go out *more* than their Single
peers would expect.

The majority of teenage couples said they had less free time
than had been the case before their move-in.

One-fourth of the Living-Together women and almost one-
third of the Living-Together men reported negative change in
their partners after they started living together. Females' responses in this area were about the same as they had been ten
years earlier. Males, however, were almost twice as likely, as
compared to 1984, to see negative change in their partners.

Almost two in five of the Living-Together respondents felt
living together was harder than they had expected. Women were

more likely, men less likely, as compared to 1984, to have these negative feelings.

Comments from Living-Together teens suggest that some feel they have given up a lot — "their teenage years" and their "freedom."

Adolescents change rapidly. Couples who start living together during this period in their lives are likely to find these changes difficult. They may discover they are growing apart and deciding they are not ready to be committed to each other.

As caring adults, we can encourage teens to delay parenting *and* moving in together until they have gotten through at least some of the changes they face as adolescents. We can help them prepare for long-term committed relationships that will enable them to cope with the changes that will continue throughout their lives.

"Justin is Hispanic and I'm white. Sometimes he has ideas about how I'm supposed to be because of the way he was raised."

CHAPTER 3

Faith and Ethnicity — Must Partners Match?

Justin is Hispanic and I'm white, and that caused clashes, basically because of his mother's bias. He came into our relationship with some beliefs about how I was supposed to be because of the way he was raised.

He always thought he was the head of the household. So when our relationship came, basically I was in charge of the kids and he was in charge of working. Then I got a job, and that was a problem, mostly because his mother thinks the woman should stay home. Justin didn't really believe that. We talked about it, and he agreed I needed to work.

The thing that really blew our relationship was him thinking, "I work hard, and I go out with my friends any time I want to," but when I went out with my friends, he'd say, "I can't believe you did this. Who were you with?" It was like if I went out, it had to be with him.

Meghan, 18/Justin, 21 (Jameka, 21/2 years)

Importance of Ethnic Background

At one time, the United States was considered a melting pot
of ethnic and religious groups. The goal appeared to be a blend-
ing of people into a homogeneous whole.

---

*Interracial marriage is much more common today
than it was 30 years ago.*

In the 60s, we realized this wasn't working well, and we
began to understand the importance of developing pride in one's
ethnic heritage as exemplified in the "Black is beautiful" concept. In spite of this change, or perhaps *because* of it, interracial
marriage is much more common today than it was 30 years ago,
and in many high schools, interracial dating is no big deal.

Both the 1984 and 1994 surveys included several questions
concerning choosing and living with persons of a different ethnic
or racial group than one's own. Responses showed changes since
1984. More teens in 1994, as compared to 1984, replied, "It
doesn't matter," when asked if they preferred to marry a person
from their own ethnic or racial group (figure 3.1). However,
more teens in 1994 felt intergroup marriage is likely to cause
problems (figure 3.2).

**"It doesn't matter whether or not I marry someone
from my own ethnic group or race."**

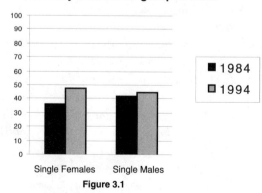

Figure 3.1

Marrying a person from a different ethnic group would "absolutely" or "probably" cause problems within a marriage.

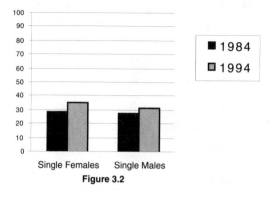

Figure 3.2

One young woman added this note to her 1994 questionnaire response sheet:

> *It wouldn't matter whether I married someone of my race, but that was a tough question to answer because you can't just look at the immediate picture. The obvious conflict would be with family.*
>
> *If the couple expects to have children, then they might want to evaluate the relationship a bit further. Kids get a lot of pressure for being from two different ethnic backgrounds.*

Although the differences are small, the increase in acceptance of marrying outside one's ethnic group and, at the same time, the increase in understanding there may be conflict appear to be healthy trends. Those who understand the possibility of problems are more likely to handle future difficulties better than those who enter into a relationship unaware that differences in family background may cause stress.

Living-Together Realities

About one-fourth of the teens living together reported their partner was from a different ethnic group or race (figure 3.3). One in five of the males and one in seven of the females found having a partner from a different ethnic group caused problems for themselves, and one in five said it was a problem for their parents. The majority reported no problem at all with differences in ethnicity.

Maurice, who is black, lives with and has a good relationship with Mitzuko, who is Korean. Maurice commented on their differences:

> *We're from two completely different worlds. It's not so much ethnic, as it's more of a social barrier. Mitzuko went to a ritzy grade school and she lived in a high income neighborhood. Me, I started off going to private schools before my parents separated. Since then, I've had a lot of hard times. I was spoiled at first, and then my folks separated, and they both lost their jobs. Our differences make life a little more difficult.*

Maurice, 20/Mitzuko, 16 (Lana, 14 months)

Maurice has a valid point. A couple from the same ethnic group may run into real difficulties if one is from an upper-middle class family, for example, and the other has spent his/her life living on welfare in a Project. Life tends to be easier for couples with similar family background, whether of the same ethnic group or not.

Is your partner from your own ethnic group or race?

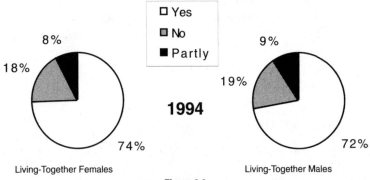

Living-Together Females   Living-Together Males

Figure 3.3

Religious Differences

In 1984, roughly half the respondents said they would absolutely or probably prefer to marry a person having the same
religious beliefs as they did. Ten years later, in 1994, that had
shrunk about ten percentage points (figure 3.4).

Marrying a person with different religious beliefs would
absolutely or probably cause problems, according to slightly
more than a quarter of the 1994 Single respondents. Ten years
earlier, a higher percentage expected problems (figure 3.5).

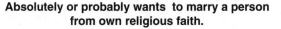

**Absolutely or probably wants to marry a person
from own religious faith.**

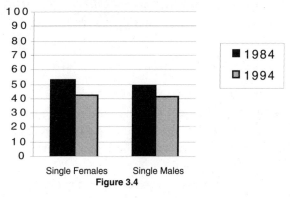

Figure 3.4

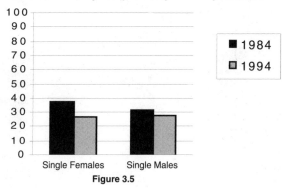

**"Marrying a person of a different religious faith
would 'absolutely' or 'probably' cause problems."**

Figure 3.5

Several interviewees, including Jessica, commented on this subject:

> Brad claimed he was a Catholic but he never goes to church. This caused a lot of problems. I always wanted him to go to church, especially with the gang involvement. He could die tomorrow.
>
> We had a big argument about getting Rodney baptized. Brad wanted it done in his mom's church, and I said she doesn't even go. I wouldn't budge on that one.
>
> He only went to church once with me. I wouldn't want to be with someone who could not respect my religion. I want my son to be brought up in a Christian life-style.
>
> Jessica, 15/Brad, 15 (Rodney, 4 months)

Importance of Religion

Only one in four of the Living-Together respondents said both partners belonged to a church, and another quarter replied that one partner did. The others, about half, reported that neither they nor their partners were church members (figure 3.6).

Does either of you belong to a church?

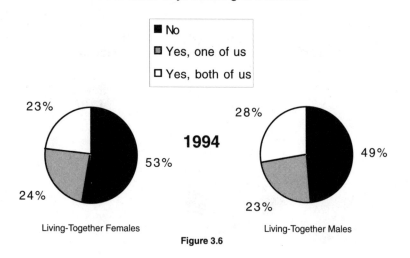

Figure 3.6

How important is religion in your relationship?

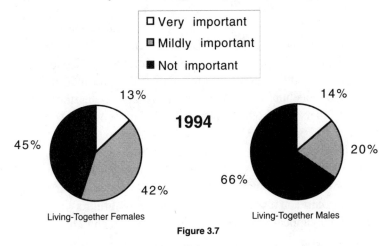

☐ Very important
▨ Mildly important
■ Not important

1994

13%

45%

42%

Living-Together Females

14%

20%

66%

Living-Together Males

Figure 3.7

As might be expected from these percentages, religion was considered very important in the lives of only a few of the respondents (figure 3.7).

He's Catholic and I'm not. It hasn't been a problem because he didn't go to church hardly ever. The only thing that bothered us was we would talk about getting married and he would want to do it in a Catholic church and I don't want to do that.

You have to go through classes, and I didn't believe in that. That bothered me.

Meghan, 18/Justin, 21 (Jameka, 2 1/2 years)

Summary and Conclusions

More teens in 1994, as compared to 1984, said it "didn't matter" whether or not they married someone from their own ethnic group or race. By 1994, nearly half gave this response.

Some of the Living-Together respondents live with a partner of a different ethnic group or race. The majority of this group reported no problems with these differences.

Fewer Single teens in 1994, as compared to 1984, care whether or not they marry a person with the same religious

beliefs, although 42 percent of both the males and the females
would prefer to marry within their own faith. Slightly more than
a quarter of the Single respondents in 1994 would expect problems from marrying outside one's faith. Ten years earlier, that
percentage was higher (females, 38 percent; males, 32 percent).

About half the respondents said neither they nor their partners
belonged to a church. One-quarter replied that one partner did,
and the others said both partners belonged to a church. Almost
half (45 percent) of the females and two-thirds of the males
reported that religion is not important in their relationship.

Churches and other groups planning programs for young
couples may want to consider these realities and concentrate on
stronger outreach along with programs meaningful to young
people who appear to place little importance on church
involvement.

While interracial and interfaith relationships are more common than they once were, some teens still feel marrying within
one's own group would be preferable. Many of those who
already are with partners of a different race or religion, however,
report no problems in this area.

No couple is perfectly suited to each other, and the fact of
same or different ethnicity or faith does not necessarily mean
they will or won't be compatible. Having similar backgrounds,
however, may increase a couple's chances for having a satisfying
life together.

CHAPTER 4

Traditional Roles
No Longer the Norm

My new boyfriend helps with the baby, but he's more, "You should do the dishes, you should clean, you should take care of the baby. I'll cut the grass, I'll take care of the car."

I don't exactly like it, but I think I can change it.

Brenda, 17/Santos, 18 (Lydia, 4 months)

Ryan's mom is always serving her husband, and that's what she thinks I should do. I don't think that way, and she doesn't understand. She says I have to think like that for things to work out between Ryan and me. He agrees.

He doesn't really say he agrees, but he expects me to do all that stuff. Before I moved in, she said I needed to help around the house. I said okay, but we never talked about my waiting on Ryan.

Conya, 19/Ryan, 21 (Liana, 11 months)

*My dad thinks he rules my mom. I want to marry
someone for love, not to be his mother or his keeper. If he
wants that, he can stay with his mama. I won't be his slave.*

Female respondent, 16

Sharing the Tasks

Love, caring, commitment, and communication are important
attributes of a satisfying partnership. Yet these positive qualities
may not be enough when the house is a mess and everybody's
hungry but no one is preparing the food—or when one partner,
often the woman, feels beaten down by too much responsibility
in these areas. A couple working together can generally
accomplish more than an individual working alone.

For many years, the accepted pattern in our society was for
the man to be the income-producer and the woman the homemaker. In an earlier time, both roles were usually full-time
occupations. The man worked many hours, probably considerably more than 40 each week, and the woman worked even more
hours as she cared for the children, kept the house clean,
shopped, prepared the meals and cleaned up afterward, and the
other never-ending tasks of keeping a home pleasant.

That pattern has changed. Today, nearly all young women
(96 percent according to this survey) expect to have paying jobs
when they don't have children and when their children are in
school.

Almost two-thirds of these young women expect to work
away from home even when they have children under age 2, and
84 percent expect to hold jobs when their children are aged 2-5.

Some teen men in the survey reported that they don't expect
to work away from home. In fact, only when their children are
under age 5 do a higher percentage of young men than young
women expect to have jobs. (See chapter 9.)

*Zaid does most of the housework because he's home all
day. He loves to clean so I leave it to him. He's a neat
freak. That's one of the biggest problems we have. He yells
at me to pick up after myself, and that's hard when you*

have a baby. He's constantly after me picking up this and picking up that.

Tameka, 17/Zaid, 22 (Chantilly, 6 months)

No longer does it make sense for the woman to take most of the responsibility for parenting and running the home. All of these tasks need to be the joint responsibility of partners just as their financial support is a joint undertaking.

Randy usually cooks and I generally do the dishes. The rest of it we split up between us. The cleaning part we talked about, but he's just a better cook than I am. He was a cook in a restaurant. That helps, and his dad was a cook.

Shanna, 18/Randy, 21 (Larissa, 15 months; Myndee, 1 week)

We take turns doing the dishes and cleaning the house. We really share everything. I guess it's because I'm easy-going and I just like to help. I don't have a job.

Kenny, 17/Misty, 18 (Damian, 11 months)

In many families, this change in male/female roles has happened within one generation. Adults who grew up with a father who supported the family financially and a mother who took care of the kids and the house now find their world has changed.

Victor never helps with the cooking or cleaning. Sometimes I don't even cook for him when I'm mad because he won't help me.

He always tells me I use the baby as an excuse, but it's real hard to clean and cook and take care of the baby at the same time. He doesn't understand that.

Trina, 16/Victor, 16 (Felipe, 3 months)

For some, accepting those changes is difficult. In the open-ended questions on the 1994 survey, 42 young people mentioned household chores as a frequent subject of their arguments. The 1994 survey asked if the wife should do most of the cooking and housekeeping. Only one in five of the Single women and one in three of the men said "Absolutely" or "Probably" (figure 4.1).

In a good marriage, should the wife do most of the housekeeping?

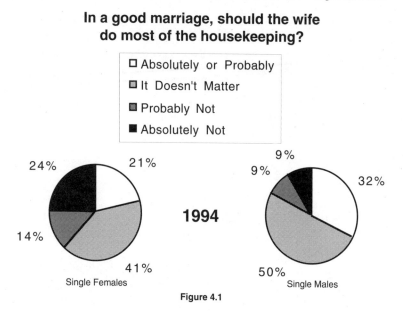

Figure 4.1

More than twice as many of the Living-Together women said they were responsible for the housekeeping tasks while Living-Together men reported a *smaller* percentage. (figure 4.2).

"In your relationship, who does most of the housekeeping?"

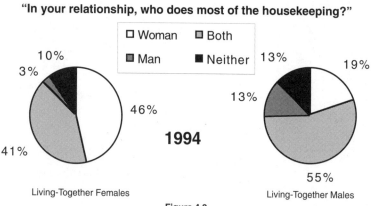

Figure 4.2

I get mad at Kent because sometimes he spends $50 a week at the lunch truck. I say, "Why don't you make your own lunch?"

*And he says, "Why don't you make it for me?" But I
can't do more. I do his laundry. I have the baby, and I
clean up our room. Kent is real messy. When he was home,
his mom picked up after him.*

Stephanie, 18/Kent, 20 (Satira, 8 months)

Majority Say Partners Should Share Housework

Dividing housekeeping into more specific tasks elicits more
information on expectations of Singles versus the realities of
those living with a partner. A majority of all the Single young
people think both partners should share the vacuuming, floor
mopping, meal preparation and clean-up, and the family laundry.

Ten years earlier, the only task a majority of the respondents
felt should be shared was cleaning up after meals. For the other
tasks, about 20 percent more of the 1994 respondents, male and
female, as compared to 1984 respondents, felt the partners
should share responsibility.

The reality of partners living together is a different matter,
although that, too, has shifted toward more sharing of household
tasks since 1984. The 1984 data for this section is based on a
survey of 81 alumnae of the Teen Mother Program, Cerritos,
California, who were asked about task responsibilities in their
first marriage or living-together partnership. No 1984 data is
available from teen men living with a partner, and nothing from
women on meal preparation realities.

---

*The realities of 1994 roughly resemble
the expectations of teens a decade earlier.*

Roughly, the realities reported also show a shift of around 20
percent between 1984 and 1994 for laundry, dishwashing, and
mopping floors, and 30 percentage points increase in partners
sharing the vacuuming (figure 4.3).

The survey realities show that for both 1984 and 1994,
expectations for *both* partners to share household tasks were

**Percentage of Single Respondents Who Say Both Partners
Should be Responsible for the Following Tasks
Compared to the Reality of Living-Together Respondents**

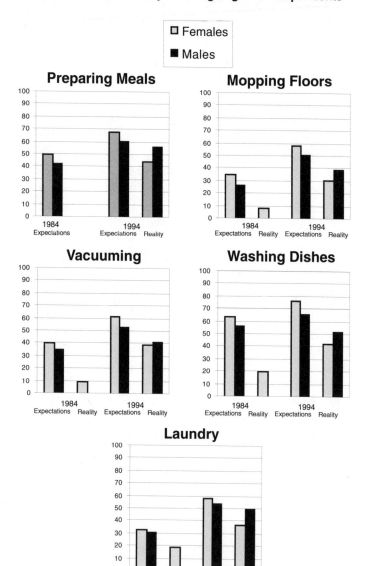

Figure 4.3

higher than the realities of Living-Together teens. However, both expectations and realities increased considerably during this period. In fact, the *realities* of 1994 roughly resemble the *expectations* of teens a decade earlier (figure 4.3).

> *Emery Dean does the housework. He makes the bed and he does the dishes. He's not too good at the cooking— he burns things, so I do most of it.*
>
> *He takes care of me if I'm sick, and I take care of him if he's sick.*
>
> April, 18/Emery Dean, 19 (Patrick, 22 months)

> *Jarrod doesn't cook because he doesn't know how except for barbecue. But he's always good at cleaning. He's a real neat person. He doesn't like things cluttered, and he never complains about cleaning. That's just him. He was raised to be a real clean person.*
>
> Anita, 18/Jarrod, 25 (Jarrod, Jr., 4 months)

Household roles are indeed changing. The realities lag behind the expectations. Probably it's *because* of those expectations, however, that the realities, too, are changing.

It is extremely important that young people discuss these concepts thoroughly before marrying and/or living together. A young woman who shares the money-earning role with her partner is not likely to look favorably at a partner who refuses to share the traditional "woman's work" tasks.

Less Sharing of Lawn, Car Care

Data was also gathered on teens' opinions regarding lawn and car care, two tasks that in many families have "always" been the man's responsibility. For these tasks, expectations and reality are not changing as rapidly as they are for the in-house jobs.

For females, the percentage thinking partners should share lawn care responsibility increased about 10 percent since 1984, but only 16 percent in each survey said this was the reality (figure 4.4). Instead, 78 percent in 1984 and 53 percent in 1994 said the man in the partnership did all or most of the yard work.

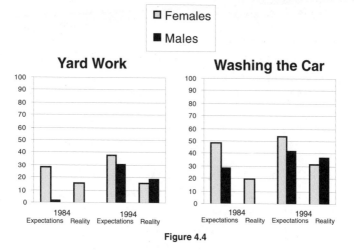

Figure 4.4

In 1994, nearly one-third of the males felt partners should share lawn responsibilities, considerably more than the 2 percent who had this expectation ten years earlier (figure 4.4). In 1984, in fact, 71 percent of the males thought the man *should* do this work.

Responses on the washing the car question show a similar pattern, although in both periods more respondents felt both partners should perform this task. Reality, again, was less sharing than expected. Only about one-third in 1994 said both partners actually shared the car-washing (figure 4.4). Nearly half of the males said they were entirely or mostly responsible for this task.

Probably many of these young people live in apartments and don't have lawn responsibilities. In fact, one in four in the 1994 survey said neither partner mowed the lawn. Others don't have a car to wash. Who does what in these circumstances isn't a particularly relevant question.

However, the trend for couples to share the tasks at home as they share income production is likely to be stronger when neither sex expects the other to be solely in charge of specific tasks. Cooking and cleaning tend to be daily jobs, tasks which in all fairness need to be shared.

Perhaps there is no car or lawn or, if there is, each needs attention only a few times a month. However, if the male is "supposed" to do those jobs, he may not be nearly as likely to think he is also "supposed" to do his share of the household tasks. A partnership is more likely to work well if neither partner expects the other to do more than his/her share of the necessary jobs.

Arkameia, who is no longer with Joshua, commented on this concept:

> *I enjoyed cooking, but I think about it now. He could have helped out. It wouldn't hurt him to put his hands in the dishwater. He could have cleaned off the table, but he thought it was a woman's job.*
>
> *Before you move in, you should sit down with the person and talk about what you expect. Who is going to do what? Make up a chart or a list. It can't just be the woman doing everything. The man can do some of the stuff.*
>
> Arkameia, 18/Joshua, 20 (Erica, 13 months)

Rating Partner's Skills

Single respondents were asked, "How important is it that the person you eventually marry/live with have the following skills . . . ?" Living-Together respondents were asked to rate their partner's abilities/actions in the same areas. Included were questions concerning cooking, housekeeping, plumbing and other repairs, and yard work.

In most of these categories, comparing the very important/ somewhat important responses with the excellent/good realities shows quite a discrepancy in expectations and behavior. Only the female responses to the cooking question were close with only 3 percent higher expectations than realities. Two-thirds of the women said their partners are good or excellent cooks. Expectations for future partners in the housekeeping, repair, and yard work areas are far higher than the realities of the reporting couples (figure 4.5).

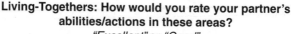

Figure 4.5

   Partners who are able and willing to perform household tasks
skillfully are likely to find their relationship goes more smoothly
than those who simply muddle through these everyday details of
living. In fact, the frustrations of everyday living can, and often
do, seriously damage relationships. Young men and women who
have an opportunity to learn these life skills are likely to have an
easier time in future relationships.

Summary and Conclusions

The traditional marriage pattern of the man earning the living and the woman caring for the children and the home has changed. No longer do the majority of teens expect future relationships to follow this division of labor.

A majority of Single respondents think both partners should share the basic household tasks. Ten years earlier, about 20 percent fewer felt the partner should share these responsibilities.

The realities are different for the Living-Together teens. For these teens, the *realities* today are similar to the teens' *expectations* in 1984. The realities don't match the expectations today, but as the expectations change, so are the realities changing.

Teens' expectations and realities of sharing lawn and car care don't match their thinking on sharing the household tasks. Males still carry the primary responsibility for these tasks, according to these young people.

Single teens were asked to rate the importance of a partner's expertise in such activities as cooking, housekeeping, plumbing and other repairs, and yard work. Living-Together teens were asked to rate their current partner's abilities in the same areas. In nearly all areas, Living-Together respondents reported partners with less expertise in these tasks than desired by the Singles group.

Teachers and others working with young people need to help them realize that their partnership will generally need to be more equal in the household task arena than was the case in many of the homes in which they grew up. Teens, male and female, need to learn the skills necessary for parenting well and for keeping a family fed and a home pleasant.

Before moving in with or marrying a partner, teens need to discuss these matters thoroughly. They need to be aware of each other's expectations, and have a clear idea about what each expects of the other, not only in the job-holding arena, but also in the home management area of their lives. *Both* are extremely important.

"He won't let me see my friends. He even gets jealous of me going to school."

CHAPTER 5

Jealousy — Love's Opponent

I feel that I've given up everything. He won't let me see my friends, my family, he doesn't like my son to see his biological father, and he even gets jealous of me going to school, and he's tried to talk me out of going. Also, I can't make simple decisions for myself anymore, like my nail color, how I fix my hair, if I wear lacy underwear, because he doesn't like me to look pretty.

Most of our arguments occur when a guy from school says hi to me, when a friend of mine wants me to spend the night or come over, and when my family wants to see me or come over. We get into these arguments because he is jealous of everyone including my son.

I don't know if our partnership will last "forever" because he lies to me and he won't believe that I'm only his and won't and haven't ever cheated on him like he has me.

Female respondent, 17

*I used to be very jealous. Once, before she got preg-
nant, we were in the mall eating a pizza and she was
looking out at nothing. I thought she was looking at a guy,
so I punched her in the leg. She got up and ran off crying.*

*The thing that flashed through my mind was my dad
hitting and fighting. Hitting doesn't solve anything. It
makes it worse.*

*From that one time when I hit her, I got over my jeal-
ousy. I knew I needed to be more sure of myself. Hitting
wouldn't help.*

Elijah, 19/Janita, 16

Jealousy is a tremendous problem with many teenagers.
Opening a class discussion on jealousy opens the floodgates for
complaints. Harrowing tales are shared of boyfriends who won't
"let" their partners go out with girlfriends, who get upset if she
visits her mother or goes shopping by herself.

Boyfriends used to come to the doorway of our Teen Mother
Program to check if any boys were there. A girl occasionally got
a little hysterical if she saw her partner talking with another girl.

Forty-seven teens responding to the open-ended questions in
the survey reported that jealousy was the subject of most of their
arguments. Thirty-eight said jealousy was one of the biggest
problems in their relationship. When asked what they feel they
have given up because of their partnership, 99 replied, "Friends,"
and 21 young women responded, "Guy friends." Two said they
could no longer "buy sexy clothes." All of these responses
appear to be related to jealousy.

Importance of Self-Esteem

*I'm very insecure about our relationship. I'm thinking
there's always somebody else out there better than me.*

*We're going through rough times, but she knows I love her
and I know she loves me.*

Jordan, 23/Danielle, 17

The ability to form an intimate relationship depends on first
developing one's own identity. A major task of adolescence is

working out one's identity. Teens who haven't mastered this task are more likely to have a problem with jealous feelings. Couples who pair up too soon may find their strong feelings for their partner interfering with the growth of their individual identities.

> *The subject of most of our arguments are over me going somewhere with people he doesn't know. He gets upset that I'm going to find someone new. I've told him, "Yes, I love you, but I need to have time with my friends. You can't keep me in the house because then I would feel trapped." Then we argue that he doesn't trust me.*
>
> Female respondent, 16

Good self-esteem comes easier if one has already achieved a firm and positive identity. The lack of positive self-esteem is often behind jealousy. If she doesn't feel good about herself, she will doubt that he really will stay with her. If he lacks self-esteem, he can't believe she can talk with, perhaps be a close friend of, another male, and still continue to be with him.

Trust is difficult for many people, and the lack of trust in his/her mate causes pain for people of all ages. Extreme jealousy can wreck a relationship.

Possessiveness and Jealousy

Anyone experiencing jealousy knows these feelings are real, no matter what their source. If jealousy occurs because one's partner is actually having an affair with someone else, denying those feelings may not be healthy. But if a person is jealous every time his/her partner looks at or talks with a person of the opposite sex, s/he needs to work toward more acceptance of and trust in that partner. Conquering this kind of jealousy is a positive step in most relationships.

Feeling overly possessive is often behind the jealous feelings she has when he talks with other girls. He may feel so possessive that he doesn't want her interacting with anyone else:

> *Before we split, during that whole time we were to-gether, it was hard. If we sat in the living room, he had to*

sit right by me, glued to me. If I moved an inch away, he'd tell me to move close.

If I answered the phone when he wasn't here and it was him, he'd give me a hard time. I was supposed to stay in my room all day long until he got home. I used to really hate that.

I didn't even have friends when I was with him. My best friend, ever since we were three years old, lives two houses down. We were best friends, but once he came along, we stopped talking. It was because he was always there, and he wouldn't let me talk to nobody, none of my friends.

I never took him away from his friends. I'd ask him not to leave with them because they all do drugs. He'd go anyway, but if my friends visited me, he'd drive them off. Every time I said something, he'd get mad real fast.

Belen, 17/Rafael, 17 (Travis, 3 months)

He used to get mad when I talked with my friends. He'd say, "I'm here. Why do you talk to your friends?" I was closed off. I never went anywhere. It was just me and him—there was no one else.

Brenda, 17/Santos, 18 (Lydia, 4 months)

After she split up with Santos, Brenda expressed her strong feelings about the need to keep one's friends:

With my new boyfriend, I still have my friends, and I go out with them about once a week. I learned when I was with Santos not ever to do that again, not to cross my friends off. When you do, after he's gone, there's nothing.

Never give up your friends. Your friends are forever, and men come and go. When they leave, you need someone to be there.

Brenda

"Looking" Is Prime Cause of Jealousy

The survey did not deal with the question of whether or not respondents have "real" reasons to be jealous. Teenagers were

simply asked, "Would you be/are you jealous if your partner . . .
a person of the opposite sex?" Questions focused on six areas of
possible jealousy: looking at, talking with, working with, attending school with, attending a concert with, and having a close
friend of the opposite sex.

Differences in degree of jealousy between the sexes were not
great. Most revealing were the numbers who said they would
either absolutely or probably be jealous if their mates "looked at"
members of the opposite sex. This would bother the *majority* of
the young people not yet living with a partner (figure 5.1).

*I'm jealous of everything. That's where most of our
problems are. I don't like him talking to any girl, and he
talks to his ex-girlfriend, Carole. He'll look at a girl, and
I'll say, "What are you looking at?"*

Sandra, 18/Troy, 21 (Violet, 16 weeks)

"Looking" can be as threatening to many teenagers as an
openly friendly relationship with another person. As one young
woman said, "Well, it depends on how he looks at her." She then
mimicked her boyfriend's come-on look which she in no way
wanted to share with another woman.

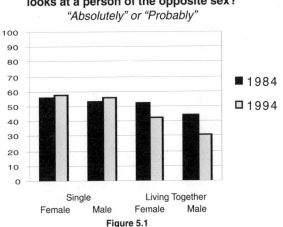

**Would you be/are you jealous if your partner
looks at a person of the opposite sex?**
"Absolutely" or "Probably"

Figure 5.1

"Looking" is the one category of jealousy which apparently is less a problem among young people currently living together as compared to Single respondents. In the 1994 study, about two in five of the females and one in three of the males in this group would be absolutely or probably jealous if their partner looked at a person of the opposite sex. In 1984, about ten percent more of the Living-Together respondents expressed jealousy "absolutely" or "positively" for "looking" (figure 5.1).

Talking with the opposite sex was not as threatening to these young people although nearly two in five of the respondents would probably or absolutely be jealous if their partners chatted with a person of the opposite sex. Changes between the two surveys were slight (figure 5.2).

> *He's real honest with me. He tells me he ran into this girl, and I jump to conclusions, and I say, "You're sleeping with her." He tells me it's not like that.*
>
> *I get mad if Daesun talks to another girl, but I think it's okay for me to talk to other guys. It's getting worse with time.*
>
> Summer, 15/Daesun, 20 (Cecelia, 9 months)

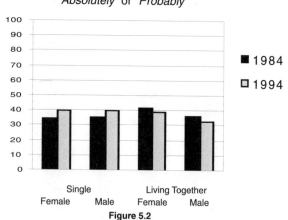

Would you be/are you jealous if your partner talks with a person of the opposite sex?
"Absolutely" or *"Probably"*

Figure 5.2

Close Friends Cause Jealousy

Daesun is an extremely jealous person. I've lost a lot of my friends because of it. I've never had a lot of girlfriends because I've always hung around men. I've lost most of these friends.

Once he hit me on the head and another time he grabbed me on the wrist, and it's all over jealousy. He has to understand I was a tomboy when I grew up, and I hang out with boys, not with girls. I share interests with boys.

Summer

When asked if they would be jealous if their partner had a close friend of the opposite sex, only one in four of the Single females (a change since 1984) said they would be jealous, while in 1994 at least half of the others, male and female, felt this would cause jealous feelings (figure 5.3).

As might be expected, having one's partner attend a concert with someone of the opposite sex would be hard for most of these young people to handle (figure 5.4).

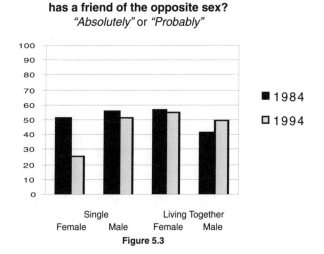

Would you be/are you jealous if your partner has a friend of the opposite sex?
"Absolutely" or *"Probably"*

■ 1984
□ 1994

Single: Female, Male
Living Together: Female, Male

Figure 5.3

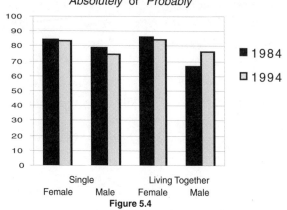

Would you be/are you jealous if your partner goes to a concert with a person of the opposite sex?
"Absolutely" or *"Probably"*

■ 1984
□ 1994

Single
Female   Male

Living Together
Female   Male

Figure 5.4

Jealousy at School

Santos and I broke up, and now I'm with Robert. He's jealous, too. He says, "Don't talk to any guys." And I have guys who are friends. I go to school with girls now, but when I go back to school, I'll be with guys, and he says I'll want to be with someone else.

There's nothing he can do—I'm going back to school. If he wants to leave because of something like that, he can. I've seen friends who, anything the guy says, they do, and I don't want to be like that.

He doesn't want me to work, and that might be part of it. After I graduate, I plan to get a job. He's already told me I don't need a job because he has money, but that's what I intend to do.

Brenda

From 15 to 21 percent of these young people said they would be jealous if their partners attended school with the opposite sex.

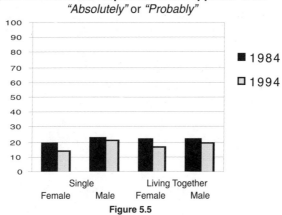

Would you be/are you jealous if your partner goes to school with a person of the opposite sex?
"Absolutely" or *"Probably"*

Figure 5.5

A young person presumably could avoid attending a concert with or having a close friend of the opposite sex. S/he might even be able to avoid "looking at" or talking with the opposite sex if s/he has a jealous partner.

But what about school? Time after time I've visited pregnant teenagers who told me their boyfriends or husbands didn't want them in school. As mentioned earlier, boyfriends sometimes came to school to see if any boys were in the classroom. Are these isolated instances, or does this actually cause a problem among many young people?

Fifteen to 21 percent of these young people said they would be jealous if their partners attended school with the opposite sex. This is a slight drop, however, from 1984 responses (figure 5.5).

Well, our education is a problem. He has graduated and I am still in school. He doesn't like me to go because of all the guys that are there. He believes that they are all after me, and want to sleep with me. We argue about this a lot.

Female respondent, 16

There are many reasons for the high number of school drop-outs among pregnant adolescents and school-age parents. In addition to financial problems and lack of child-care, a mate's jealousy may be a big factor in the decision to quit school.

One-fifth of all male respondents say they would be jealous if their partners attended school with males. This means many of their young partners may simply quit attending regular classes. Those districts which offer a self-contained program as an alternative for pregnant teens, however, are likely to find some of these young women participating — young women who otherwise would be school dropouts.

Many school districts across the country offer no special services for pregnant teenagers and school-age parents. Of those which do, the trend appears to be away from separate programs and toward integrating special services into the comprehensive high school.

Offering special services in these schools gives these young people the opportunity to stay in their own schools and still receive the much-needed special services, certainly an advantage for many students.

However, an even better approach for school districts would be to provide both a self-contained class *and* the special services in the comprehensive school. If the goal is to keep young people in school — which translates into preventing future dependency on welfare for many of these young people — the school administrators need to consider the culture in which these students live. Continuing in school can be an important step toward growing out of an overly possessive relationship. For some, being able to attend a self-contained class during pregnancy is the bridge they need to take that step.

Working Often Provokes Jealousy

Yes, there's a lot of jealousy. I really don't like her talking or seeing other guys. I don't like her working with or going to school with guys.

Wes, 20/Traci, 16 (Elias, 20 months)

See chapter 8 for a quote from Traci concerning Wes' unwillingness to work, and how difficult it is for Traci to support them and their child.

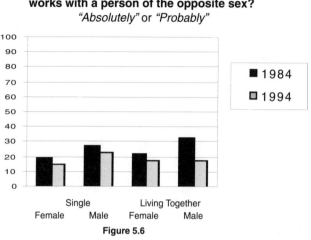

Would you be/are you jealous if your partner works with a person of the opposite sex?
"Absolutely" or *"Probably"*

Figure 5.6

Ten years ago one in five of the females and from one-fourth to one-third of the males said they absolutely or probably would be jealous if their partner worked with a person of the opposite sex. That percentage has decreased during the past decade, especially among Living-Together males (figure 5.6).

A high percentage of these young people expect their partners to hold paying jobs at some point. They know two paychecks are required in many families simply to pay the bills. Hopefully, their jealous feelings will decrease as they mature and gain more positive self-esteem.

Karina — Case Study

Karina is an especially attractive Hispanic 16-year-old married to Vincent who she says she dearly loves. Karina's father and mother are still together, but her father has always had other women friends including one with whom he has two children. Karina blames her father's infidelities for her extreme jealousy of Vincent. She explained:

We had a fight lately over the fact that I don't trust him. When I was 2 months pregnant, I found my husband talking to another girl on the phone. And last December I caught him again, and by this time Vincent was my husband. I told him, "This is it." I said, "You know what, the second time you do it, you are gone, you are history. I won't tolerate being married to you."

So it happened again a year later. I called her on the phone and asked, "How many times have you guys talked?"

"Only twice."

I said, "He's married and has a kid, and I suggest you stay away from him."

She said, "I don't want any problems, and I have a boyfriend."

I told Vincent, "I don't need you. I don't need your money. I married you because I love you, not because I need you. You can leave whenever you want, but I keep my kid." I said, "You can decide right now what you want, whether you want to be with me and only me, or you can leave me and go with whoever you want."

And he said, "Well, what's wrong with talking with other girls on the phone?"

That really pissed me off because he could have said he was sorry. To him, his morals, that's not wrong, but to me it is real bad. I said, "If you want to be with me, you don't talk to other girls."

I said "This is your last chance. The third strike and you're out."

Then I found a number on his watch, a girl named Sally. I asked, "Who is that?" But I wrote the number down.

He said, "She works there, she's pregnant, and she is married." So I believed him.

Later I called, and this guy answered the phone, named Curt. I said, "This number came up on my phone bill."

He said, "This is Curt and my roommate Sally."

I got real pissed off and I came home and told my husband, "You have to tell me what's going on."

*I got real mad. This was just two days ago. I got real
mad at him and told him all these things, that he didn't
know what commitment was, just laying it on him. If I
didn't love him so much, I wouldn't put up with it, even if I
only suspected. I talked to my mom and she said, "No
matter how hard you push, he isn't going to confess."*

*So he came home from work. I told him, "I feel a lot of
the problems we have is because I don't trust you. So what
I'm going to do is lay my guard down. I'm not going to
check on you. I'm going to let you be, just like nothing ever
happened. If you decide to mess up on me, I won't find out
right away because I won't be checking, but when I do find
out, you'll really get it. I'm going to try to trust you. You
know what I like and what I don't like. If you walk down
the street and talk to a girl, that's bad."*

*I was working for a month, and I had a whole lot of
guys want to take me out even though they knew I was
married. I told them I have a husband, I have found the
light of my life. I told my husband, "You aren't the only
one. Don't think that you're better than I am. How would
you feel if I did the same thing you're doing?"*

*He said, "I'd get mad." He says it's different because
I'm a girl. We have had this argument so many times, but
now we're doing so much better. If he messes up with me
he isn't ready for commitment.*

*He used to be very very jealous when we were going
out. Then I got pregnant and he stopped being jealous.
Now I'm about 20 pounds overweight and sagging.*

Karina, 16/Vincent, 20 (Saulo, 7 months)

Summary and Conclusions

Many teenagers appear to be extremely jealous if their
partners talk with or even look at people of the opposite sex. The
majority of survey respondents said they would be jealous if
their partners "looked," and nearly two in five had the same
feelings if partners talked with members of the other sex.

Even school attendance causes problems for many of these

teenagers. The result often is a pregnant teenager or a school-age wife who drops out of school because of her mate's jealousy. School counselors and teachers need to exert special effort to encourage these young people to stay in school. Districts which offer a self-contained class *as a choice* for pregnant teens may have better success in keeping some young people in school. Requiring students to attend a special program because of pregnancy or marital status is illegal, but offering choices to students is good education practice.

Anyone who has experienced jealousy knows these feelings are real, no matter what their source. If one's partner is having an affair with someone else, it's certainly normal to be jealous, to be hurt. The individual needs to deal with those feelings and with the situation. But a person who is jealous every time his/her partner pays any attention to a person of the opposite sex, as Karina relates, needs to work toward more acceptance of and trust in that partner. Conquering this kind of jealousy is a positive step in most relationships. Suggestions for teenagers working on this problem are offered in *Teenage Couples—Caring, Commitment and Change.*

The "cure" for jealousy many times is improved self-esteem on the part of the jealous person. (Karina's final comment, "Now I'm about 20 pounds overweight and sagging" is a revealing statement.)

Jealousy causes pain for many people, both adults and teenagers. Learning to control jealous feelings, to show trust, respect, and caring as part of their total love for each other, is a major learning task for teenage couples.

Trust and jealousy are not compatible, and trust is a basic ingredient of a good relationship. For many teenagers, building that trust is difficult.

The most important thing a counselor, teacher, parent, or anyone else can do for a teenager is help him/her develop positive self-esteem. Helping him/her get a good education and develop salable job skills are valuable steps toward reaching this goal. In the process, the young adult is likely to find jealousy is no longer the problem it may have been.

CHAPTER 6

Partner Abuse — Killer of Love

He used to hit me, but no more. He knew that if he hit me and hurt me, he'd go to jail, and it wasn't worth losing me and the kids.

The first time he hit me was when I was living with his mother. He hit me a lot when I was pregnant with both of the kids. After the kids were born, I told him, "No more hitting or messing around." I said there just could not be more of it. It was time to grow up. I could do better by myself. And he knew I meant it. Things changed.

Candi, 20/Jeremiah, 21 (Jakela, 2; Kamika, 1)

The biggest problem in our relationship was his drinking. He likes to tell me what to do and he likes to use threats such as "I'll break your car window." Once he ripped the phone cord out of the wall saying that I was going to call the cops on him. I really loved him and I still

care. I love the part of him that's caring but I hate the
ugliness that the alcohol caused.

Female respondent, 16

Every 15 seconds a woman in the United States is beaten.
Studies of high school and college students conducted during the
1980s reported rates of dating violence ranging from 12 percent
to 65 percent. When I was teaching teen parents, I was aware of
a disturbing amount of violence in my students' relationships.

Some Teens Condone Violence

People are not for hitting. However, a dishearteningly high
percentage of young men *and* young women in the survey
tolerate partner abuse under certain conditions.

The good news is that the research reported here shows less
acceptance of men beating women than was reported in the 1984
survey.

In the 1984 study, when asked, "How do you feel about men
hitting their partners?" one-third of the teen men and one-fourth
of the teen women said either "It's okay," "Sometimes it's
necessary," or "It may happen when he's angry or drunk." By
1994, the percentage tolerating violence ranged from 11 percent
of the Single females to 21 percent of the Living-Together males,
still a frighteningly high acceptance of abuse (figure 6.1).

I think it's okay. A person could have a very bad temper
and they have to let it out.

Female respondent, 14

A still larger proportion in 1994 (one-third of the women,
one-third of the Single men, and one-fourth of the Living-
Together men) said it was either okay for a wife to hit her
husband, is sometimes necessary, or may happen when she's
angry or drunk. An even higher percentage of the Living-
Together group condoned women hitting men in 1984.

People hitting people is not right whether the hitter is male or
female. The fact of the male's greater size and strength, however,

means men can physically hurt women a great deal more than women can hurt men. The reality is that one-fourth to one-third of the women in this country are beaten at some point by their partners or dates, but far fewer men are physically abused by women. For these reasons, this discussion will focus on the attitudes toward and the reality of men abusing women.

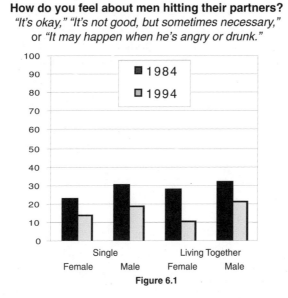

How do you feel about men hitting their partners?
"It's okay," "It's not good, but sometimes necessary,"
or *"It may happen when he's angry or drunk."*

Figure 6.1

For Many, Reality Involves Hitting

The above statistics are based on the attitudes of young people. The reality, according to the 1994 survey, is that about one-third of the Single women and even more, two in five, of the Living-Together women have been hit one or more times by a date or partner (figure 6.2).

Eighteen of the 54 women I interviewed in 1994 reported having been hit by a partner. Some of them had managed to get out of the abusive relationship, while others said the hitting had stopped because their partner knew they would leave if it didn't.

There was a time when all we did was fight and fight and fight. At first it really surprised me, and then I started fighting him back because I was just as frustrated as he was.

It has stopped. We were constantly fighting. I guess it stopped when we moved out of his parents' house. One thing that really bugged me was if he was hitting me, they didn't say anything, but if I was hitting him, they would tell me to stop. He's stronger than I am so he would hurt me more.

I could have gone home, but I didn't want my mom to say, "Well, I knew you were going to come back home." I didn't want to go back to hear that. I wanted to prove to her that I could do it.

Carman, 16/Caesar, 21 (Sergio, 2 years)

We lived together for two years. Then he started to treat me bad. When I was pregnant, he used to hit me. I didn't do anything about it for at least two years, and it was hard. We were living at his parents. When I moved in, I was barely 14. I had known him for about a month.

At first everything was going all right, but he used drugs, and I didn't know. Then he became jealous and he started hitting me and I didn't do nothing about it.

Then when I got pregnant, I decided I didn't want to be with him because of my baby. I've had a bad life. I'm with my parents now.

His parents would tell him not to do it, but he went right ahead, and I guess they didn't care. He wouldn't let me go to school. He'd say I would be with somebody else.

I saw my parents twice during those two years because Manual didn't let me come over here to see my friends. I was upset but I couldn't do anything because he'd hit me. So I'd say, "All right, I'm not going."

Lourdes, 16/Manuel, 15 (Katrina, 4 months)

Teenage Couples—Caring, Commitment and Change includes other young women's accounts of being abused by a partner. For some, the abuse started when they were extremely young.

Has a date or your partner ever hit you?
"One or more times"
NOTE: Information from 1984 refers only
to Living-Together women who have been hit.

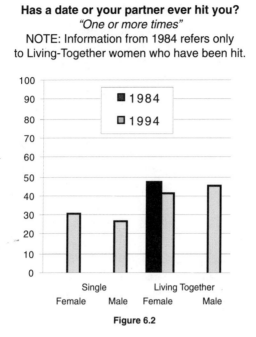

Figure 6.2

Reasons for Staying

Leaving appears almost impossible for some. The reasons women give for staying in such a situation include:

- She is afraid of what the man would do to her and her children if she tried to leave him.

- She thought all along that the man would change and stop beating her.

- She may have had no one to turn to and she didn't know where to go for help.

- Perhaps she had no money and no safe place to go.

- Often a woman believes she is at fault and that she has no worth as a person.

- She may also have believed she had to keep her family together at all costs no matter what the pain and the danger.

Support Groups Can Help

Mary Marecek was for many years the Program Director of Respond, Inc., in Somerville, Massachusetts, a suburb of Boston. Respond, Inc., offers counseling, legal aid, support groups, and emergency shelter for battered women.

"The most important thing we can do to stop family violence is help people realize that beating and abuse are not all right under any circumstances, not when he's drinking, not when he's on drugs, not because his mother or father beat him," she pointed out. "That's when we begin to see some changes—when women who were trying to find excuses and reasons for the beatings finally realize there are no excuses. Only then are they able to let go of the guilt, the idea that if she were a better wife, he might not beat her."

Ms. Marecek talked about the need for teenage women to internalize this concept, to understand that violence is wrong. If the first time he grabs her and pushes her, she says "No," she is saying to him, "That's not okay. You have to make some changes."

"This puts the focus in the right place which is on his behavior," she explained. "The earlier this happens, the better."

Counseling the Abusers

Counselors with Respond, Inc., work closely with Emerge, a counseling agency in Boston for abusers. An abusive man is likely to continue to be violent and to escalate the violence unless he receives help, but abusers often don't seek help voluntarily, according to David Adams, Program Director for Emerge.

"Eighty percent of our clients are court-referred, and these clients actually do better than voluntary clients, mostly because they stay in our program longer," he explained. The court-referred clients are ordered into a 48-week program, while the volunteers tend to stay for a short period, perhaps eight weeks, then drop out after the initial crisis is passed.

The Emerge program includes extensive contact with the clients' victims, and about half of the clients are living with the women. "Even if we can't help the batterer change, we help empower the victim," Adams said.

"We find that the adult men we work with overwhelmingly got started as abusers in their earliest teenage relationships, and that generally the violence escalated with each successive relationship. And, sadly," he continued, "the younger the victim, the less likely she is to recognize she is being abused."

While there are many programs across the country for batterers, very few take teenagers. "What teens need is basic information about relationships," Adams pointed out, "and they need quite different kinds of counseling than do adult men."

A few schools offer violence prevention programs, and materials are available for use with groups. *Relationships without Violence: A Curriculum for Adolescents* by Anne Stewart Helton is available from the Texas Gulf Coast Chapter of the March of Dimes. (See Bibliography.) The purpose of the five-session curriculum is to prevent violence in dating and among family members, and it is designed for students in grades 9-12.

Preventing Teen Dating Violence: A Five-Session Curriculum for Teaching Adolescents and *Respect Can't Be Beat: Peer Leaders Manual* are available from the Dating Violence Intervention Project, Cambridge, Massachusetts. (See Bibliography.) Edited by Carole Sousa, the curriculum has three major components: preventive education, intervention through school-based victim groups and perpetrator groups, and peer empowerment. The material is designed to be teen-taught, with one male and one female leading the group.

School programs can help teens understand that violence is *not* part of a good relationship and, at the same time, give young people the skills to prevent abuse toward themselves and others.

Case Study — Arkameia

A young woman wanting to get out of a violent relationship may find counseling helpful, as Arkameia did. Her parents died when she was 9, and she moved in with relatives. When she was 13 she started seeing Joshua. Now 18, with a 13-month-old daughter, Arkameia describes her experience. Joshua is in jail, and she is trying to make a new life for herself and her daughter.

Joshua and I moved in with one of my friends when I was 15. I wasn't pregnant when we moved in together.

Joshua stayed at home a lot at first, and I liked that, that he didn't work and spent his time with me. But then he started changing.

He started hitting me, perhaps three months after we started living together. It was hard—I'd be scared but I accepted it. I never said anything. It was like I let him do it, like I gave him permission, like I thought that was what made him happy. He hit more and more often.

But now I look back and it was like I gave him all that advantage — like when he'd hit me and I never said anything, that was like filling his head up with "I can do it."

How did I change? It was my daughter. After Joshua went to jail I'd look at Erica and think, she's without a dad now, and I was without my parents. I want her to graduate, but how can she if I don't? So I went back to school. I didn't think I'd do good, maybe I'd get Ds or Cs. My first report card I got As, and I went home and thanked Erica.

I feel better about myself now. I'm a sophomore, and I get straight As. I was out of school almost two full years, and also like when I was still in school I was never there. I'd always miss school to be with Joshua.

I went to counseling and this lady helped me out. She made me realize a lot of things. Like if you let things go on, you get used to it and it's your way of life. I got used to him hitting me. I got used to staying up until 4 in the morning waiting for him.

Counseling did a lot for me. Expressing myself more, not holding everything in. You have to let your feelings out. You can't hold them in. You see, when my parents passed away I wouldn't talk to nobody. And the first person I talked to was Joshua, and he turned around and did all this stuff to me so I closed up again.

You have to want to get out of the situation . . . I was obsessed with Joshua for a long time, but when I decided I wanted something different, the counselor helped.

Summary and Conclusions

About one in five of the men and one in eight of the women in the survey said it was either okay or sometimes necessary for men to hit their partners, or it may happen when they're angry or drunk. Even more young people ten years ago appeared to condone violence. In that survey, one-third of the teen men and one-fourth of the women said either "It's okay," "Sometimes it's necessary," or "It may happen when he's angry or drunk." Having one in eight of the women and one-fifth of the men in the current survey giving these answers is still a disheartening reality.

An even higher percentage of respondents condone women hitting men.

One-third of the women respondents reported having been hit one or more times by a date or partner. Eighteen of the 54 women interviewed reported having been hit by their partners. Violence is a tremendous problem for many young people.

Women who are abused often feel they are at fault. They may also believe they must stay in the relationship for the sake of their families. Joining a support group can help women understand they are not alone, and that they do *not* deserve to be hit.

Those who abuse women are not likely to stop unless they are involved in counseling. Sometimes through counseling they are able to change. If this doesn't happen, the women involved in abusive situations need help in getting out, in realizing the abuse is not their fault, and that they have a right to a better life.

A necessary part of this "right" is the ability to support herself and her children. Again, education and job skills are the root of the solution. Combining education, job skills, and positive self-esteem may provide the direction she needs.

Mary Marecek is the author of ***Breaking Free from Partner Abuse*** (1993: Morning Glory Press), which stresses the fact that no one deserves to be hit, and that no one should remain in an abusive situation. The book is written directly to women who are victims of abuse. It is easy to read and provides an excellent approach to a difficult subject in Family Living or other classes.

Included in the book (page 29) is the following poem by Ms. Marecek which is reprinted with her permission:

hope

After you once raised your voice to me
Then your hand
Then your fist
I lost respect
    for you
    for myself
    for us . . . what we once were
And never will be again.

I live in hope
    that you will change
    that I won't feel guilty
    that we will be happy
    that you will stop drinking
    that you will die.

My hope is a pipe-dream
I live in hope.

Adults who work with and/or care about teens must do everything possible to help young people, men as well as women, understand that *no one* deserves to be hit. Hitting is not right, and hitting absolutely does not belong in a love relationship.

Young men must understand that hitting their partners solves nothing and is likely to wreck the relationship. Young women must also understand that hitting one's partner is absolutely not done.

Most important, young women must understand that abuse is not something they deserve, and when abuse happens, *they must get out of the relationship.*

CHAPTER 7

Your Parents or Mine? Living with In-Laws

*We were in an apartment when we first got married.
When we moved here it was an adjustment. It was hard.
Every once in a while if Judson and I get in an argument,
my mom goes, "What's wrong? What's wrong?" I get in the
middle all the time because Judson complains to me, my
mom complains to me. I get mad, very upset. I'll fight with
my mom, then I'll fight with him. I try to stick up for my
mom and I try to stick up for Judson.*

*I don't like it, but I'm always there. My mom and I are
real close so we talk about everything. I guess trying to
explain to both of them how I feel can help, but they both
get insulted. Then I try to patch it up and everybody
gets mad.*

Aracely, 18/Judson, 27 (Chianti, 18 months)

*Usually I'm real neat, but his mom's house was hard
because there were so many things everywhere. She rarely*

cooked for herself because she was rarely home. We got in
a lot of fights. The first week or two, we ate together. When
the fighting started, we'd eat by ourselves and she'd do her
thing. We worked around the cleaning thing.
*   When me and Jordan would argue, she'd get very mad.*
She was real protective of Jordan, and she would
automatically take his side.

Danielle, 17/Jordan, 23

In some cultures, a woman's mother-in-law rules her home.
Mothers-in-law are often stereotyped as unkind, sharp-tongued
women who make their daughter-in-law and/or son-in-law
miserable.

Many, many parents-in-law, of course, are loving, caring
people who do not fit this stereotype. Nevertheless, living with
one's partner in either his or her parents' home can be stressful.

Okay to Live with Parents?

Respondents were asked, "How do you feel about a young
couple living with either his or her parents?" In 1994 roughly
one in twelve of the Single respondents thought this was a good
idea. Less than half of the others said this would be okay "until
we save some money." The rest, 50 percent of the females and
44 percent of the males, answered "I'd rather not" or "I'm totally
against it" (figure 7.1).

Yet 85 percent of the women and 72 percent of the men
already living with a partner had lived with other people at least
part of the time since they started living together. The majority
had never lived by themselves as a couple. Many, as couples, had
lived with his parents, her parents, or both (figure 7.1).

Many young couples must live with parents in order to
survive financially. Those who can't handle the stress and decide
to move out may have to cut their education short in order to
earn enough money to pay the bills. If they have a baby, paying
those bills on one parent's salary may appear impossible. Those
couples who agree that living with parents is all right "until we
save some money" are facing and accepting their reality.

Single: How do you feel about a young couple living with either his or her parents? *"Okay"* or *"Okay until we save some money."*

Living-Together: *"My partner and I have lived with extended family or friends all or part of the time we've been together."*

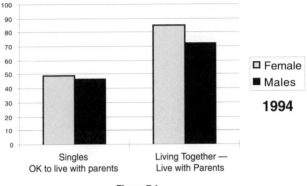

Figure 7.1

Relationships with Parents Explored

Teenagers who already have a poor relationship with their parents may find it especially difficult to continue living with them after marriage or to move in with a partner and his/her family. In the survey, teenagers were asked about their feelings toward their mothers and their fathers.

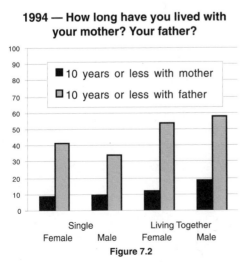

Figure 7.2

In 1994, teens who lived with a partner were more likely, compared to Single respondents, to have spent less than ten years living with either mother or father. (With whom they lived is not known.) More than half of this group had lived with their father less than ten years (figure 7.2).

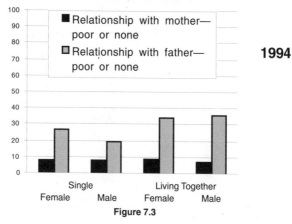

How would you rate your relationship with your mother? With your father?

Figure 7.3

Teen men from the Living-Together group, as compared to the Single males, were more likely to say they have a poor or no relationship with their father. In fact, more than one-third of the Living-Togethers, both male and female, said either they had no relationship with their father, or the relationship was poor (figure 7.3). This data suggests that some teens may be more likely to form an early living-together partnership if they do not have a good relationship with their fathers.

Arguing About In-Laws

Open-ended questions in the survey for Living-Together teens included "What is the subject of most of your arguments?" and "What are the biggest problems in your partnership?" Eighty of the 362 who responded to these questions listed in-laws as the subject of most of their arguments. An additional 24 listed family as one of their biggest problems. Only money outranked in-laws as the subject of the most arguments between partners.

Comments from interviewees often included reference to in-law problems:

I always stay in our room because I don't feel at home. I want to get out as soon as I can. He's a mama's boy and he's spoiled. My opinions don't count. Whatever she says, she convinces him to do. They butt into everything, and when we fight, they always want to know what it's about.

Conya, 19/Ryan, 21 (Liana, 11 months)

Caesar's family never ate together. Everybody kind of ate whenever they felt like it. I like eating together. My mom always made sure we ate together but they don't.

Carman, 16/Caesar, 21 (Sergio, 2 years)

My boyfriend and I have tried to live with his parents. They were too controlling and treated us like we were in elementary school still. They didn't respect us as far as us being a little family just starting out.

Female respondent, 17

Lack of Privacy

Crowded households may be particularly stressful for a young couple. Some couples don't even have a room of their own. Those who do complain of paper-thin walls and of siblings who allow them no privacy.

I don't feel I have any privacy here. When Maurice's mom wants to come in, she'll knock. Then she opens the door and comes on in. If I'm dressing, she may say, "I'm sorry," but she stays there and keeps talking. My grandma didn't even do that.

Mitzuko, 16/Maurice, 20 (Lana, 14 months)

Sometimes we're in our room and have the door shut, and my mom or dad just walk in without knocking. Michael tells me to talk to my parents, but I can't. I get terribly embarrassed, and I can't talk to them.

Teresa, 18/Michael, 22 (Taylor, 8 months)

We have no privacy. If I want to hug him and kiss him, I have to go in the living room. Me and my mom share a room, and my boyfriend has to sleep outside. Our home is very crowded. I wanted to go back to his mom's house

because there is more room over there, but my mom says,
"Just go ahead and go, but leave the baby."

Arlene, 14/Alfonso, 16 (Sylvia, 4 months)

Acquiring more privacy may be as simple as installing a lock
on the door to their room. The "lock" can be a hook and eye
attached to the door and door frame, if the host parents allow it.

Help — Too Much or Too Little

My mom wants control. She wants to tell us how to
raise our son, and we tell her she's not the mom of Elias,
so back off. And if Wes and I get in a fight, of course my
mom takes my side because I'm her little girl. Wes doesn't
like that, but I tell him the reality is we have a roof over
our heads because of my mom.

Traci, 16/Wes, 20 (Elias, 20 months)

Parents who have already reared their children often want to
give advice on child-care to their live-in son or daughter. The
young parents are not likely to appreciate this "help."

Sometimes they try to tell me how to raise the baby.
"Put a sweater on him." "Do this." "Don't do that."
I don't want to give him soda and candy, and they do
anyway. I don't tell them not to because if I do, they
get hurt.

Conya

Other young wives are frustrated because they don't feel
needed. They want to "keep house" but find his/her mother is
taking care of everything.

Having him move in was weird. At first we had our own
place, and his mom was living with us. I didn't really like it
and I felt uncomfortable. Suddenly I couldn't do anything
around our apartment. She did the cleaning and cooking,
and I wanted to do it. She did everything and I couldn't do
anything. We didn't really talk. I'm kind of shy.

Teresa

Some young women spoke of moving in with parents-in-law and feeling as though they were expected to act as maids to the rest of the family.

I didn't know his family when I moved in. I wasn't pregnant then—I moved in because I had so many problems with my parents.

It was hard because they wanted me to do everything. His parents wanted me to cook for them and clean the house like a maid. I was living with them for free.

I went to school for two or three months, and then I dropped out. I'd just stay home, cook for him, clean for him. I'd help him with his homework when he came home from school.

Lourdes, 16/Manuel, 15 (Katrina, 4 months)

Developmentally, adolescents are likely to think mostly of their own concerns. If a partner moves in, mom, dad, and siblings are supposed to take it in stride.

Of course, mom, dad, and the siblings have their own concerns, and adding another teenager to the household usually is not high on their list of preferences.

I did my best, and I tried to remember it was my choice to be there. I felt my parents shouldn't have to support the baby. It was Caesar's responsibility to support both of us, and my parents were having lots of financial problems.

His parents were nice but sometimes they bugged me because they wanted me to clean up after them. I only cleaned up after us. Sometimes I felt like I had to because we weren't paying rent. We were just paying for food.

Carman

A 16-year-old in anyone's home may find it easy to feel "like a slave" while a mother-in-law may be determined not to take on the work of caring for another "child." Good communication and compromise are essential.

A contract set up before move-in time might prevent frustration later for everyone concerned.

Communication Skills Needed

Couples of any age may find it easier to bond together and
form a satisfying relationship if they are able to live by themselves. If they don't have this opportunity, how can they develop
that satisfying relationship even as they interact with other
family members, and sometimes with many people living in the
same household?

Communication skills are important. If the young couple can
discuss difficulties with other family members, solutions may be
found. If either of the young persons can't or won't talk with the
others, problems may become bigger and bigger. Some families
find that regular family meetings help:

*Living with my family is hard because there's two
mothers in the house, my mother and me. It's like we're
both trying to order everybody around.*

*We have family meetings every week. My mom and I
haven't gotten along as well because of the baby. My other
two sisters live with us, and sometimes I try to boss them
around and my mom doesn't like that. So we all sit down
on the couch with my step-dad and we talk about our
problems. Then we talk with the individual with whom
we're having problems.*

Daisy, 16/Wayne, 17 (Mecailea, 9 months)

Coping with extended family living usually demands good
communication between the couple and with other family
members if the relationship is to continue.

Summary and Conclusions

About 85 percent of the young women and 72 percent of the
young men already living with partners started their lives together by living with his parents or hers or with friends. Many of
these young people did not want to move in with in-laws, but
they felt they had no other choice.

Many of the young people complained about their situations,
but others spoke of arrangements which, while not what they

might prefer, were working. Lack of privacy, over-supervision by parents, and unfair division of household chores were among problems mentioned.

An additional factor is the poor relationships with fathers and mothers reported by many of the survey respondents. A higher percentage of Living-Together respondents, as compared to the Single participants, reported poor relationships with their fathers. Combining an already-poor relationship with parents with the move-in of one's partner may explain some of the difficulties encountered in these extended families.

Teachers and others working with teens can help them learn practical problem solving, communication skills, and conflict management which can help solve some of the perennial problems that arise in extended family living. Judicious use of the same three skills between partners can also be a tremendous help as they deal with the changes which occur in themselves and in their relationship.

Each couple together with their families needs to consider carefully all the ramifications of the living-together choice *before* they decide to move in with his or her parents or with friends. They need to face the fact of some conflict being inevitable.

If everyone involved can discuss together *before* the move-in their expectations concerning division of work, privacy, financial arrangements, house rules, and the other aspects of communal living, their chances of coping well with an inherently difficult situation will improve. A pre-marriage contract can help families set up guidelines for a successful living-together arrangement.

If everyone works together to develop a simple contract of expectations before the move-in, life is likely to be easier for everyone. An example of such a contract is included in *Teenage Couples—Coping with Reality,* chapter 3. For additional insight into extended family living, see *School-age Parents: The Challenge of Three-Generation Living* (1990: Morning Glory Press).

Extended family relationships are like all relationships. The three Cs—caring, concern and consideration of each other's feelings—help *stop* the problems before they become unmanageable.

*"We feel education is the only way
we'll get where we want to go."*

CHAPTER 8

On Moving In —
And Dropping Out

Education has a big effect. I resent him because I dropped out to have his child and then he left me!
Female respondent, 16

I want a better job, but all I have is my high school diploma. Most of the jobs I want take more than that.
Being a respectable person is important. If you don't respect yourself and others, you won't make it. Respect yourself and others and they'll respect you back.
Jeremiah, 21/Candi, 20 (Jakela, 2; Kamika, 1)

He dropped out before we met but I dropped out because I wanted to be with him more. Our relationship has ended since he was sentenced to ten years in prison. I have learned that I needed this to show myself I deserve better and my education and self-esteem are important to me.

> *Advice: Take your time and make sure you don't have to count on your partner—be independent! Don't let yourself get to where you can't leave him no matter what he does.*
>
> Female respondent, 17

Importance of Education

Earning ability is considerably dependent on education and job training. Traditionally, teens who married before finishing high school were likely to drop out. Girls who were pregnant were actually pushed out of school. This practice became illegal in 1972 with the passage of Title IX Guidelines which are applicable to all schools receiving any federal funding. However, many districts continued the practice of expecting pregnant and parenting teens to leave school, or at least to transfer to an alternative school where the quality of education might not be as high.

Today, many living-together couples and pregnant and parenting teens continue their high school education. Many others, however, do not. The dropout rates in many of our schools are tragically high.

Most young couples who live together want as much independence as possible. The longer they depend on their parents for financial support, the less likely they are to have the independence they want. Some teens try to solve this problem by dropping out of school and going to work. When they do, they may be facing a lifetime of poverty because of their lack of education and job skills.

Other couples realize the importance of getting an education and manage to cope with living with his or her parents as they do so. If they have a child, they may be even more convinced of their great need for more education.

> *We're both in school. He helped me go back to school with encouragement, and he goes to night school at our community college. He graduated high school and we'll both continue our education. We feel education is the only way we'll get where we want to go.*
>
> Female respondent, 17

*Advice: Finish school, make what you can of yourself,
and DON'T rush your life. You'll have plenty of time for
everything later.*

Female respondent, 16

Dropping Out Because of Moving In

During the 16 years I taught teen parents, I was thrilled at the
numbers who came back to school after dropping out. At least 40
percent of the students in our program (based at an alternative
school) had dropped out before enrolling with us, half of them
before getting pregnant. Over and over I heard, "I have to have
an education now for my baby."

At the same time, through our extensive outreach program,
we were aware of a disheartening number of young people who
did *not* return to school. Many of these young people were living
with their partners, and sometimes I'd hear, "I'm not in school
because he doesn't want me there."

I would also hear of boyfriends who had dropped out because
they felt strongly their responsibility to support their partners and
children. And there were also boyfriends who refused to get a job
or go to school.

---

*More than a third
of the young women in the survey
said their partners had
actually dropped out of school.*

Several questions in the survey dealt with this topic. "How
much has getting married or living with your partner changed
your school attendance? Your partner's school attendance?"

One in four respondents, both male and female, reported that
their school attendance dropped and/or they dropped out of
school while living with a partner (figure 8.1).

*This was the year for me to graduate, but I won't be
graduating because my ex-husband told me I couldn't go*

On moving in, did school attendance change?

When you moved in with your partner, did your school attendance change?

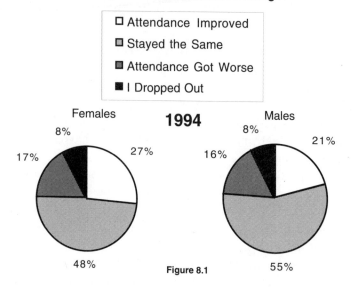

☐ Attendance Improved

▨ Stayed the Same

▦ Attendance Got Worse

■ I Dropped Out

Figure 8.1

When you moved in with your partner, did your partner's school attendance change?

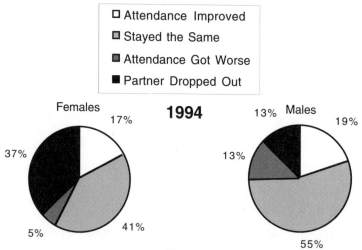

☐ Attendance Improved

▨ Stayed the Same

▦ Attendance Got Worse

■ Partner Dropped Out

Figure 8.2

*back to school unless I had a baby-sitter for our daughter.
And at the time he wasn't working.*

*When me and my partner got married it was because I
was pregnant plus I wanted to get out of my dad's house
and we were in love.*

*We mostly would fight about money or him being on
drugs which always led to fighting about money.*

*No, nothing is forever. I feel we fell out of love. The
drugs got to him so bad that it made our relationship even
worse.*

Divorced respondent, 19

Even more reported that their partners' school attendance had dropped or their partners had dropped out of school. More than a third of the young women said their partners had actually dropped out (Figure 8.2).

Most of these respondents were in school at the time of the survey. Undoubtedly, many more young couples have dropped out of school together, and thus are not represented in these statistics.

The lack of interest in education exhibited by one-fourth of the respondents appears to fit with the results of the "Do you expect to work if . . ." survey described in chapter 9. This data shows about one in four of the males among the Living-Together respondents saying they do *not* expect to work while they have children under 5.

Effect on Relationship

Teens who were living with or had lived with a partner were asked about the effect of education on their relationship. Most of the 362 teens who responded to this open-ended question felt there was no effect. One in ten of these respondents, however, had brief comments. A couple of the comments referred to the difficulties of doing "everything":

*It's hard to try to finish school, be a mom, wife, and I
try to have a part-time job with a little extra income.*

Female respondent, 16

A few young people were clear about the value of education:

Education has a very big effect because we have
children and we need to better ourselves.

Female respondent, 16

A few comments from or about male partners were positive toward education:

My boyfriend gets upset with me when I don't go to school.

Female respondent, 15

When I was with her, I only came to school three full
days my freshman year. Now that I'm not with her in my
junior year, I'm passing everything, and I'm in school
almost every day.

Male respondent, 17

Jordan, 23 and employed, was concerned about Danielle's sporadic attendance at school:

If she doesn't go to school, I say, "Danielle, you've got
to go to school."
I try to tell her, and she says, "You aren't my father, you
can't tell me what to do."
So I back off. I say, "You do whatever you want to do."
She's mature in some ways and immature in others.
Her aunt called me the other day and said Danielle
wasn't going to school. I talked to Danielle, but she tells
me immediately, "You aren't my father."

Jordan, 23/Danielle, 17

Partners who Nix Education

Thirty-three female respondents among the 362 Living-Together teens responding to the open-ended questions wrote of partners who didn't want them in school, partners who felt threatened by the young woman's interest in education, and other negative attitudes toward school attendance. The following comments are typical:

We fight because he feels I try to act like I'm better than him because I go to school and he doesn't.

He never felt like going to school so I was the one who paid for it because he wouldn't let me go either.

He was a dropout, had no life, no job. I was going to school and he was jealous because he knew that I would have a life ahead of me.

He doesn't want me to go to school because he's jealous, but I'm not going to let him ruin my dreams.

I plan on getting a good job because of my training, but my partner is having trouble finding a job because he dropped out.

What is happening here? Why are so many of these young men uninterested in education, either for themselves or their partners? Why would these young women choose to have a relationship and live with partners whose values appear to be quite different from theirs? Answers to these important questions are beyond the scope of this project.

Summary and Conclusions

This study provides information on the probability of teens' interest in school decreasing after they start living with a partner. One in four of the respondents, male and female, reported that their school attendance went down or they dropped out after moving in with a partner. A higher percentage (42 percent) of the partners of female respondents had either dropped out of school or their attendance had dropped.

These are important findings for teachers and guidance counselors. First, let's remember that if one in four doesn't attend school regularly and doesn't expect to work, that leaves three in four young people who do continue their education and who expect to work to help support their families. This study does *not* suggest that all young men or even all young men living with partners, prefer to loaf their lives away.

The survey does illustrate the need for changes in our education system, in our families, and in our culture, changes which possibly could result in almost all young men and young women becoming responsible members of families and of society.

Those who work with teenage parents have an important role in this goal because change happens more easily in the formative years. If babies and toddlers develop good self-esteem and the knowledge that they can effect changes in their lives, they are more likely to grow up to be adults who do not need to move in with a partner or make a baby too soon, people who will understand and act on the need for a good education and the development of job skills.

Teachers and guidance counselors, at whatever grade level, must emphasize these goals, must teach and guide young people with caring, and must use techniques that work. There is no simple solution, but we cannot afford to ignore *any* young person. We have an especially important challenge to help those youth whose needs are most difficult to meet, and who truly need the most assistance in order to cope well with their lives.

CHAPTER 9

Men Who Don't Work And Women Who Do

*He dropped out of school in the 9th grade, and I'm
almost out of high school and planning on going to
college. And he doesn't like that my education is higher
than his. The biggest problem is he's lazy and doesn't want
to work.*

Female respondent, 17

*I get help from the families and from the government.
With so little money, we spend it only on the things we
have to have. There isn't any extra money to worry about
for movies or junk food.*

Elijah, 19/Janita, 16

Time after time, in open-ended questions, teens living with a
partner complained about lack of money. Money, many said, was
the cause of many of their arguments. Asked about the biggest
problems in their relationship, money was frequently listed.

Being together all the time is a problem. We get bored.
We don't have a lot of money so we can't go out and do this
or do that. We get frustrated with each other.
The money plays a big part—we don't have a car so we
catch the bus. Will the baby be warm enough? Do we have
enough formula? So we usually just stay home.

Tameka, 17/Zaid, 22 (Chantilly, 6 months)

Often young women spoke of partners who couldn't find a
job, didn't have job skills, and/or simply did not work.

Lack of Money = Arguments

When asked the subject of most of their arguments, money
was mentioned by 99 of the 362 Living-Together respondents
who completed the open-ended questions. Money was mentioned
more often than any other topic, generously outranking in-laws,
friends, and household chores, other often-mentioned subjects of
arguments.

In addition, 45 of these respondents listed money as the
biggest problem in their partnership, again outranking every
other topic mentioned.

Money—that's the #1 thing we argue about. I pay the
bills, the utilities, cable, all the luxuries with the money I
get from my job. He pays the rent, the credit cards, and his
car payments. I like to go shopping, and he says I buy
stupid things.
We each have our own money, and I probably spend too
much of mine. Once the bills are paid, I go buy what I
want.
We don't put our money together now. We will when we
get married—and then I'll have more money to shop with!

Katelynn, 17/Nathan, 20 (Daron, 21/2 years)

Eighteen who were living together reported they were not
married because of lack of money.

Most young couples are short of money. Teenage couples are
even more likely not to have enough money to cover their needs.

Couples who choose to continue their education may be
particularly short of cash, and those who don't expect to work
can anticipate many money problems.

In chapter 8, quotes from numerous young women describe
partners with a serious lack of interest in school, and, for some,
in working.

Whose Job Is It?

This study shows that teens' viewpoints of wage-earning
responsibilities have changed since 1984. At that time, a scant
majority of males and 70 percent of the females said both
partners should be responsible for their financial support. In
1994, both sexes' expectations of both partners earning money
had increased nearly 20 percent (figure 9.1).

Marlene and Jeremy understand that each needs a career in
order to have the life they want:

> *Jeremy graduated last year from high school, and he's
> working now. After I graduate this spring, I'll probably get
> a job this summer because we're sort of low on money. We
> need to save up for college.*

Marlene, 16/Jeremy, 19 (Amber Marie, 7 months)

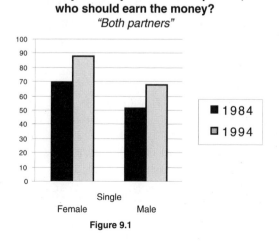

**If/When you marry or live with a partner,
who should earn the money?**
"Both partners"

Figure 9.1

Opinions on Working

Several questions in the survey asked respondents about their expectations of working at different periods in their lives. Questions included "Do you expect to work outside your home if you have no children? If your child is under 2 years of age? If you have children aged 2-5? All children are in school?" Respondents were also asked if they expected their partners to work during these periods.

Partial comparative information is available from 1984. Only about half as many women in 1984 as in 1994 expected to work while they had children under two. Men were far less likely in 1984 to expect their partners to work away from home either when they had children under two or when all children were in school (figure 9.2).

Not Everyone Expects to Work

In the current survey, six out of ten of the young women expect to work away from home while they have children under 2. More than eight in ten of the women expect to work while the children are aged 2-5. All but four to six percent of the female respondents expect to work away from home when their children are all in school (figure 9.2).

When there are no children
or the children are in school,
a higher percentage of teen women than teen men
expect to work away from home.

The puzzling thing about these findings is the number of young men who do not expect to work outside their homes whether they don't have children, their children are under 2, aged 2-5, or are in school. If they have children under 2 years of age, 19 to 26 percent of the male respondents say they either won't work, probably won't work, or "It doesn't matter." Almost as many, 14 to 23 percent, give these negative responses when asked if they expect to work while they have children aged 2-5.

Seven to 10 percent do not expect to work when they have no children or their children are all in school.

In fact, when there are no children or the children are in school, a higher percentage of women as compared to teen men, expect to work away from home. The higher percentage not planning to work in each case refers to young men already living with a partner, and many of these young men are already fathers (figure 9.2).

Expectations have changed along gender lines. In fact, in the 1984 study, men were not even asked if *they* expected to work, and women were not asked if they expected their *partners* to work. Conventional wisdom at that time was that the man was simply expected to hold a paying job. That was his role. Men were only asked if they expected their *wives* to work, and women were asked about their own plans for working away from home.

Phrasing of the questions in surveys administered only ten years apart gives insight into changing viewpoints on gender roles. The teens' responses to these questions give even more insight.

Comparing current responses of females and males to the questions concerning working expectations for themselves and for their partners shows a somewhat surprising pattern. The percentage of young women in both groups who expect both themselves and their partners to work is higher than the young men's expectations for themselves and their partners. That is, men are less likely to expect their partners/wives to work than the women themselves expect to work. Men also are less likely to expect to work themselves than their partners/wives expect them to work (figure 9.3).

Looking at the current survey, one wonders who will support the children—assuming that both parents are responsible for their sons and daughters. For some, of course, the father may stay home and care for the children while mom works. Only about one in ten of the 1984 respondents considered this an acceptable possibility, but in the current survey, one-third of the females thought this would be okay, and even more of the single males agreed (figure 9.4).

Do you expect to work outside your home if you have no children?

"Yes" or *"Probably"*

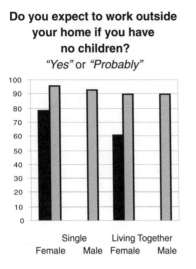

	Single		Living Together	
	Female	Male	Female	Male

Do you expect to work outside your home if you have children under two years of age?

"Yes" or *"Probably"*

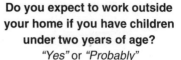
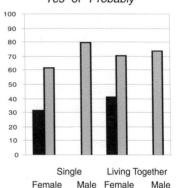

	Single		Living Together	
	Female	Male	Female	Male

■ 1984
▨ 1994

Do you expect to work outside your home when your children are 2-5 years old?

"Yes" or *"Probably"*

Do you expect to work outside your home when your children are all in school?

"Yes" or *"Probably"*

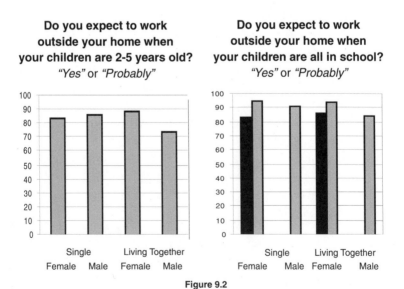

Figure 9.2

Do you expect your partner to work outside your home if you have no children?
"Yes" or *"Probably"*

Do you expect your partner to work if you have children under two years of age?
"Yes" or *"Probably"*

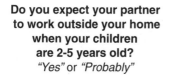

■ 1984
▨ 1994

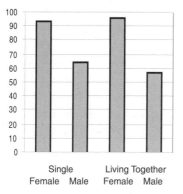

Do you expect your partner to work outside your home when your children are 2-5 years old?
"Yes" or *"Probably"*

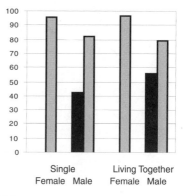

Do you expect your partner to work outside your home when your children are all in school?
"Yes" or *"Probably"*

Figure 9.3

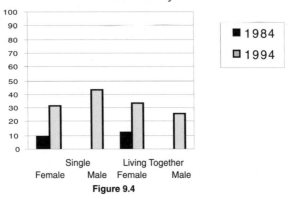

Okay for man to stay home while partner gets a job?
"Yes" or *"Probably"*

Figure 9.4

Possible Explanations

It is likely that some respondents, both male and female, plan/
hope to be home with the children while their partner provides
financial support. And of course this will be possible for some
couples.

> *I've had a job, but we agree I don't need to work right
> now. I had summer jobs—I was a secretary, and I learned
> to type 80 words a minute. I stopped working in my sixth
> month of pregnancy.*
>
> *I'm going to be home for awhile after I have this one.
> Then I'll go to college. I want to spend the first year with
> our children. That's important.*
>
> Selia, 19/Enrique, 19 (Riquie, 11 months)

Another possible explanation for the number of males not
expecting to work is that for parenting respondents, the question
might have been interpreted to refer to their current lives. Some
may understand the importance of getting an education and job
skills now instead of working. The extent of this interpretation is
not known because the questions were not designed to elicit this
information.

Our education takes up a lot of our time. If we weren't going to school, we could work more hours for extra money, but without school, we'd always have minimum wage jobs which wouldn't help us out in the long run.

Male respondent, 17

The non-working response may be a realistic answer because of the lack of job opportunities.

Another untested possibility is that some respondents plan to earn income by working at home, and interpreted these questions literally as simply asking about place of employment. In such cases, the answer was "No" because they didn't expect to work *away from home.*

For some young people, sadly, the non-working response may have been considered a realistic answer because of the perceived lack of job opportunities.

In some inner city areas, the unemployment rate for teen males is estimated to be as high as 80 percent. For these young men, some of whom may have no working role models at home, getting and keeping a job may appear unlikely.

Zaid doesn't work. My stepdad is trying to get him a job. He's 22, and he doesn't have much education at all. In the past he's had little odd jobs here and there.

I'd like him to get a job, something to keep him busy. I think he needs something to keep his mind occupied and to boost his self-esteem.

Tameka

Some young men (and women) simply don't want to work:

I know I have to get a job, but I don't really want one. I've worked at several jobs, but I didn't like any of them.

Wes, 20/Traci, 16 (Elias, 20 months)

Traci commented on Wes' unwillingness to work:

I feel a lot of pressure. I'm supporting Elias by myself. I buy the diapers, everything. I get real frustrated because Wes isn't helping out.

The more I pressure Wes, the more he isn't going to get a job. He worked at a canning plant here, but he's not one to get up early in the morning. It was a 7 A.M. job, and he didn't like to get up that early.

When I had to get to work at 5:30, he'd take me, and then he wouldn't make it to his job. Then one day he didn't call in, and he got fired.

                                                                Traci

These are possible explanations for the numbers of young men not expecting to work. Each suggests special education and job training needs for the young people involved.

Parenting Education for Mom *and* Dad

Too often the young people I've interviewed, respondents who have completed open-ended questions, and young people with whom I've worked have included individuals who must take responsibility for the children, cooking, keeping house, *and* either working or going to school while the partner is *neither* working nor attending school. Generally in these situations, the person handling most of the responsibilities is the mother. Even if dad doesn't have a job or attend school, he may not choose to work at home:

Sometimes the house would be clean when I'd come home from school because he wasn't working. Other times, I'd come home and he wouldn't even be up yet. It bothered me that he wouldn't work, or go to school, or help around the house.

Yelling and screaming didn't help. Sometimes I'd sit down and say, "I feel real mad when you don't help me," or "I'm real tired tonight. Could you give Jacari a bath this time?" Or trade off with the chores. "You do dishes

*tonight, and I'll do them tomorrow night." Sometimes he
pitches in.*

Angelica, 18/Ricardo, 18 (Jacari, 3 years)

Angelica and Ricardo are no longer together.

If dad isn't working and mom is, he needs to take primary
responsibility for the home and the children. This probably was
not the pattern for his parents, and he may not have learned the
skills needed for these tasks. These skills are essential, however,
in today's world. If both parents work, they need to share the
tasks at home.

First, all young people need to learn the art and skills of
parenting. Parenting needs to be shared by mom and dad, and
each needs to be able to parent alone when necessary, whether
it's during the hours the other parent is working, or during times
s/he may be a single parent. Good parenting in this sense also
involves learning the consumer and homemaking skills which
can make life go better for a family.

The traditional marriage when dad earned the living and mom
took care of the kids and the house won't be the norm for most
of today's teenagers. Whatever their beliefs about equal marriage, economics and the goal of good parenting demand *two*
highly skilled and caring parents. In most families, both are
needed to produce enough income, to parent the children, and to
do the household tasks.

Special Needs Job Training

The survey included no questions concerning the kinds of
jobs these young people might want. Some, perhaps, are planning to work at home, and therefore don't expect to work away
from home. Since the numbers of people working at home is
increasing steadily, job training courses and counseling need to
include a component of entrepreneurship.

Teachers and counselors need to be careful not to oversell the
joys of running one's own business, however, because this is
likely to be a rather unobtainable goal for many young people, at
least in the near future. Guidance in small business operation

must not replace, but be in addition to, solid job skill-building.

Additional and intensive guidance is imperative for youth who don't plan to work because they don't want to or are convinced there are no jobs for them. As mentioned before, several young women in the survey spoke disparagingly of mates who do not/will not work. Several of the couples I interviewed expressed the same problem. A couple of young men flatly stated that they didn't want to work.

We need to help these young people realize the joys of being financially independent, the satisfaction of going to work regularly, and earning enough money to support one's family. Only then will job training make sense to them.

Training and guidance for young women need to include emphasis on learning non-traditional (for women) job skills because pay for these jobs is likely to be significantly higher than in the traditional "woman's work" jobs.

Money Management Help Is Needed

Even if one partner, or both together, make "enough" money, the couple's problems continue unless they learn how to manage that money in a way that is satisfying to both of them. As mentioned above, over and over again in the open-ended questions from the survey, Living-Together teens mentioned money as the cause of most of their arguments, and as their biggest problem.

Interviewees also frequently discussed financial difficulties:

I try to get half the money, but Alfonso says I'm tight with it. I'm not—I just know how to spend money. What I get, we need.

When he gets money, he wants to spend it. "Let's get that, let's get this." But I say the baby needs things. I say, "Let me have half the money, and you take the rest." He agrees sometimes, but other times it's "No, I have to fix my car. I've got to do this or that." He does buy the baby's diapers and other things she needs.

He gives my grandma $50 a month. When we first moved back here, he thought she wouldn't want him here.

It was crowded already and he didn't want to make it worse. Sometimes he'd go back to his house because he didn't want to be a burden. At first my grandma would say, "We don't have enough of this or that," but now that he's giving her money, it's better.

Arlene, 14/Alfonso, 16 (Sylvia, 4 months)

The survey results provide additional information about this subject. Among the teens not living with a partner, a majority (females, 71 percent; males, 57 percent) said married or living-together partners "absolutely" should agree on how they spend money. Among those already living together, however, only a minority (females, 36 percent; males, 45 percent) "nearly always" agree on this important issue (figure 9.5).

Do you and your partner agree on how you spend your money?

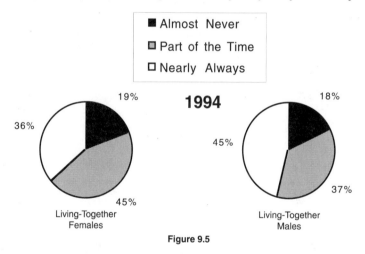

■ Almost Never
▣ Part of the Time
□ Nearly Always

Figure 9.5

Joe's parents paid for his stuff when he was in high school while my parents didn't help. I always yell at him because I don't think he knows how to budget money.

Before we were married, I had to pay for my car insurance. I'd save a little each week. He pays for it with one check instead of saving for it. That means his whole check is gone that time. I gripe about it, and it goes in one ear and out the other.

Erin Kathleen, 18/Joe, 21

Two-thirds of the Single respondents felt that being a good money manager was important, but fewer, about half, of those living together rated their partners as good or excellent money managers (figures 9.6, 9.7). The apparent lack of expertise in money management among the others suggests that teens need help in learning to budget and to handle money wisely.

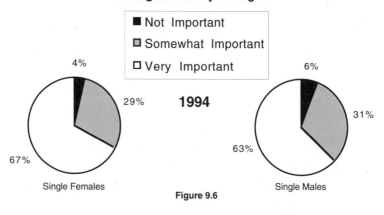

How important is it that the person you marry be a good money manager?

■ Not Important
▨ Somewhat Important
□ Very Important

1994

4%
29%
67%
Single Females

6%
31%
63%
Single Males

Figure 9.6

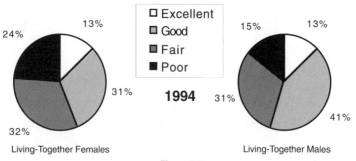

How would you rate your partner's money-management abilities?

□ Excellent
▨ Good
▨ Fair
■ Poor

1994

13%
24%
31%
32%
Living-Together Females

13%
15%
31%
41%
Living-Together Males

Figure 9.7

Money was a problem. We always fought about money.
We didn't have that much. We were getting AFDC for the
three of us. That's how we survived.
    We disagreed on how to spend the money. Almost all of
our money went to rent. What we had left Ricardo wanted
to buy tapes for himself or new pants for himself. He
wanted his own spending money and he didn't want me to
have any money for food. He'd call his family in another
state, and that was expensive. We didn't do any kind of
budget. I think it would have helped if we had budgeted.

Angelica

Teachers, counselors, and group leaders can make a difference
in young people's lives by helping them become intelligent
consumers. Individuals and couples who understand the additional spending power and heightened satisfaction that comes
from wise spending are likely to practice the planning and
budgeting that can provide them with greater joy in their
spending and saving.

Teenage Couples: Coping with Reality offers a plan for
budgeting, and guidelines on shopping for food, using credit, and
other aspects of intelligent consumership. Emphasis is placed on
the importance of developing a spending plan which satisfies the
people involved rather than attempting to follow a model budget
set up by someone else. Negotiating agreement on priorities is
important for all couples.

Summary and Conclusions

The traditional pattern of men working and women staying
home no longer is typical. According to this survey, a majority,
six in ten, of teen women expect to work even while they have
children under 2. More than eight in ten expect to work while
their children are aged 2-5, and nearly 95 percent of the women
plan to work when their children are in school.

Only while their children are under five do more young men
than women expect to work away from home. Even during this
period, 19-26 percent of the male respondents do not expect to

work away from home. Seven to 10 percent do not plan to work when they have no children or the children are all in school.

This shift in men's working plans probably has occurred for several reasons. Some men will be the homemaker while the female partner provides financial support. Some men may plan to work at home and interpreted the question as focusing only on jobs outside the home.

Some young men have no hope of getting a good job. They may have no working role model at home and see few opportunities in their environment. Such a situation translates too easily into lack of incentive for job training and productive work.

Our role as teachers, counselors, and caring others is multi-faceted. All young people need to learn the art and skills of parenting and of home management because these tasks will be shared by both partners. Both partners also need high-quality career planning help and job training. Helping young people become productive citizens is an expensive and time-consuming task. Not helping them is a much more expensive approach.

In addition, the issue of child-care is an extremely important part of this whole subject. Obviously, quality child-care is essential for infants, toddlers, and preschool children whose parents work away from home, and, just as obviously, quality care is not widely available.

Also important is after-school care for children and supervision for teens whose parents are not available. Latch-key kids are often in jeopardy, yet this survey reinforces our knowledge that most parents will have jobs away from home.

Our society is facing a multitude of family-value issues. This study is further evidence of the needs of our children, and the responsibility of the community in providing services for families who cannot afford to be with their children full-time.

Financial problems faced by many teenage couples are severe and can be devastating to a relationship. *All* young people must be encouraged to obtain job skills and to prepare for a career. Most will need to produce income throughout most of their lives, and the more skills they develop, the more choices they will have. *Having choices* can add significantly to the quality of life.

CHAPTER 10

"HE'S MY BABY, TOO" — TEEN DADS *ARE* INVOLVED

We're trying to be responsible just like my parents were with us. They were going to separate a couple of times, but they stayed together because of the kids. If things don't work out for us, I'll try to stay together for the kids. They don't need to be with a single parent. I don't want to answer those questions about where is he or where is she?

Jeremiah, 21/ Candi, 20 (Jakela, 2; Kamika, 1)

Having a baby changed my life. It keeps me from running around, doing guy stuff. I miss it. I go out once in awhile and play ball. I used to drink a lot, but I don't any more. I stopped because of Damian.

We do hardly anything together anymore. Sometimes we watch TV and play cards together. Before Misty got pregnant, she worked at the swimming pool. We used to go swimming together and go down to the river, walk around,

*watch people. We don't do stuff like that anymore. We're
more concentrated on Damian.*

Kenny, 17/Misty, 18 (Damian, 11 months)

*When the baby was real small we were getting up a lot.
I was getting real tired, real sick of it, and grumpy. Yes,
we'd have arguments and scream. We'd get pushy. We
wouldn't hit each other, but it was getting kind of violent.
Then we thought about the baby and decided that wasn't
the thing to do. So we ended up waiting until we settled
down before we talked about the problems. That helps.*

Anita, 18/Jarrod, 25 (Jarrod, Jr., 4 months)

Effect of Child on Relationship

More than half (381) of the Living-Together respondents had
a child at the time of the survey, and one-third of the females
were pregnant. However, only 211 of the parents were living
with their child's other parent. Four hundred ninety-five of the
Single respondents also had a child.

> *Parents from both groups reported changes
> in their relationship with the other parent
> after the child was born.*

According to researcher Jay Belsky, Ph.D., "Of the three
million couples who become new parents each year, nearly half
will not find the joy and happiness they envisioned." Belsky's
research, as reported in *The Transition to Parenthood* (1994:
Dell) focused on older couples, mostly those in their late 20s.
Usually these couples had made a deliberate decision to have a
child. Generally they had enough money to live comfortably by
themselves.

Yet many of the 250 couples he studied found the three years
after their child's birth to be difficult. For some, instead of
strengthening their marriage, the baby's presence seemed
somehow to pull them apart.

What effect, then, must a baby have on a couple not yet out of school, a couple who must depend on parents for financial support, a couple barely even considering the idea of marriage?

Mostly we argue over the kids—me taking care of the kids. Sometimes I don't be watching them or pick up enough time with them, stuff like that. Or Candi will come home from work and I may not have cleaned up, and that's an argument.

Jeremiah

It is not surprising that some teen couples reported that their child has had a negative effect on their relationship. The surprise is that so few appeared to feel this way.

Parents from both groups reported changes in their relationship with the other parent after the child was born. Almost half of the Singles group and half of the males and two-thirds of the females of the Living-Together respondents reported the child had a *good* effect on their relationship. Many of the others said the child had no effect.

Of those not living with a partner, about one in six said the child had a bad effect on the relationship. Males and females in the Living-Together group, however, differed in their responses.

Effect of child on your relationship with other parent?

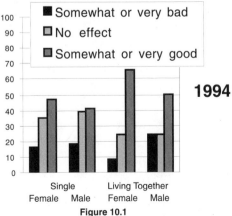

Figure 10.1

Only one in ten of the young women said their relationship with
the other parent was worse because of the child, while one in
four of the Living-Together fathers felt this way (figure 10.1).

Majority of Dads Are Involved

*With a kid, it's a lot of stress. You have to just hang it
out, and don't be an absent parent. It takes two to tango,
and it takes two to parent a kid.*

Traci, 16/Wes, 20 (Elias, 20 months)

Of the 69 young men in the Living-Together group, 32 have a
child, but only 17 live with their child and his/her mother.
Nevertheless, only three are not involved with their child. The
other 12 see their child occasionally, with four of the 12 in daily
contact (figure 10.2).

*More than two-thirds of the Single fathers
spend time with their child.*

Eighty teen fathers in the survey don't live with a partner. The
stereotype of teen fathers who don't live with their child and his/
her mother is one of non-involvement. If the young couple is not
together, the dad must have skipped out. He must not care about
his child.

Reality for some young fathers is quite different. Almost three
in four of the Single fathers report spending time with their child,
at least occasionally. In fact, four of these Single fathers have
sole custody of their child.

Nearly all of the young fathers in this survey were enrolled in
school when they participated. It is possible that teenage fathers
attending school may be more involved with their children than
adolescent fathers in general. However, Nigel Vann, Project
Officer of the Young Unwed Fathers Pilot Project, Public/Private
Ventures, also reported a high rate of involvement between
young fathers and their children. Of the 228 fathers included in
their early project research, 70 percent reported seeing their
children at least once a week (*Teen Dads*, page 13).

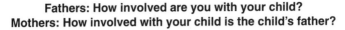

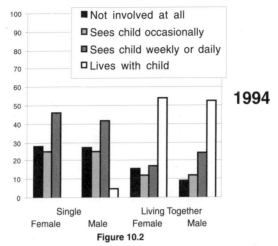

Figure 10.2

Most Dads Want More

In interviews and in other conversations, many teenage fathers told me they grew up without a father, and they didn't want their child to have that experience. They want to be involved. They want to help parent their child. In fact, they want more involvement than they have. More than half of the Single fathers and three-fourths of the Living-Together dads wanted more involvement with their children (figure 10.3).

Enrique, who is married to his son's mother, talked about the reasons he wants to be with his son and the things he hopes to teach him:

I want to teach my son everything I didn't learn from my father. That's why I work so hard. It isn't just for the money. It's for the discipline, the responsibility.

So now I can say as my child is growing up and he gets to the age where he's ready to work—I can say he should go through this, too. I'm going to have him doing all kinds of chores. And I won't pay him for everything. You can't buy responsibility.

Enrique, 19/Selia, 19 (Riquie, 11 months)

Involvement for some means far more than sharing baby care. Involvement in parenting may lead to a serious change in life style:

> *One day me and Angela were walking home from the store. Some guy came swerving into the sidewalk, and I gestured at him. He made a U-e in the street and came back and pulled out a gun.*
>
> *I've been reflecting since then. If he had shot me, then Angela and the baby would have been alone. Or he could have shot the baby. Maybe I shouldn't have gestured.*
>
> Juan, 18/Angela, 16 (Vaneza, 7 months)

Mothers Report on Dad's Involvement

About 800 young mothers are represented in this survey. Three hundred forty-nine live with a partner, but only 211 live with their child's father. How do these young women feel about the father's involvement in their child's life?

For some, nearly one-third of the Singles and one in six of the Living-Together group, the father simply is not involved. The rest of the Singles group report that their child's father sees him/her either occasionally or daily. More than half of the Living-Together mothers report living with their child's father, and the others, 29 percent, say the father sees the child occasionally or daily (figure 10.2).

Information is not available as to how many mother/father pairs are included among the parenting respondents. That is, the information from the young fathers and the information from the young mothers probably does not generally come from a mother and father of the same child. In fact, if the young mothers in the survey are typical of national statistics on the age of the fathers of teen mothers' babies, more than 70 percent of their partners are adult men, and therefore are not represented in this survey.

In spite of the lack of responses from parenting pairs, females' responses are much like the males, both in the percentages of fathers who see their children regularly, and in the mothers' feelings toward more involvement for the fathers. The same proportion, 55 percent, of the Singles, females and males, would like their child's father to be more involved in his life. For those living together, 62 percent of the mothers would like more involvement (figure 10.3)

Fathers: Would you like to be *more* involved with your child?
Mothers: Would you like your child's father to be *more* involved with your child?

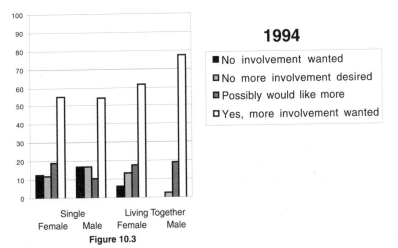

Figure 10.3

Majority Provide Financial Support

I want to give Davina and Valizette more. Sometimes that's a problem for me—to be in somebody else's home and be taking from them. Sometimes I feel like I'm not providing. I get down. I want to give her more.

Johnny Angel, 19/Davina, 19 (Valizette, 11 days)

Some fathers do not provide financial and other support:

I ask him all the time why he won't be involved with his baby, but he pretty much does what he wants to do and he won't listen. There's a lot of fighting because he won't do this and he won't do that.

On and off André works, but he provides no financial support. When it's convenient for him, he'll pick Keisha up

*and feed her. If his friends are around, he doesn't do
anything for her. If I turn around and say, "André, this is
our kid and you aren't doing anything," he has a fit.*

*I ignore him because he's not around very much. I don't
want to go back with him, but he's still the father of my
baby. I want more than anything for him to straighten up
and be with the baby, but I know once he leaves, he'll just
disappear. My father was never around when I was little,
and my mom never told me anything bad about my dad. I'll
do the same with Keisha.*

Disiree, 17/André, 18 (Keisha, 4 months)

The majority of fathers not living with the mother provide
some financial support. Only one in six of the Living-Together
male respondents report paying no child support, and most of
these young men are still in school. A little more than one in four
of the Living-Together female respondents report no support
from the fathers (figure 10.4).

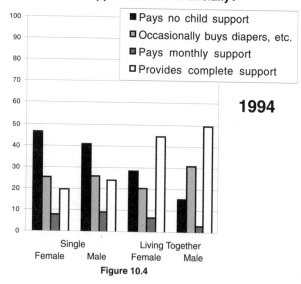

**Fathers: To what extent do you support your child financially?
Mothers: To what extent does your child's father
support him/her financially?**

Figure 10.4

Mothers reported receiving a little less child support than fathers said they provide. However, respondents, as mentioned above, are not likely to be partners to each other.

It is important to note that 20-50 percent of the fathers providing complete financial support for the child is a much higher percentage than is generally assumed to be true for the babies of teenage mothers.

Teens in the survey, those without children as well as the young parents, generally have traditional views about a couple's joint responsibility toward any children they have together. The overwhelming majority think that when a man impregnates a woman, he should take responsibility for the pregnancy and the child. Respondents also believe it is important for a child to live with both parents. (See chapter 1.) Many of these young men are living by those standards.

What Is Dad's Role?

When dad is around, what role does/should he play? Even if mom is willing to be the primary caregiver, children generally benefit from a strong relationship with their father. Time after time, as mentioned before, teenage fathers have told me they plan to "be there" for their child because they never knew their own fathers. "I don't want that for my child," they say.

Ideally, the parents have a stable, long-lasting relationship, but this is not reality for many of today's teen parents. Seventy-one percent of the babies born to teenagers in the United States are born to single mothers.

Most often, the young mother is the primary caregiver for the child. When this is the case, the young man may assume that he has no right to see his child if he provides no financial support. Laws vary from state to state, but generally this is not the case. Unless the court decrees otherwise, he has a right to spend time with his child whether or not he can provide financial support.

At the same time, of course, the father is liable for half the support of his child until the child is 18 years old. If dad is still in school and is earning no money, he can't pay, but he will be

liable for that support as soon as he can get a job. His child is his
legal responsibility whether or not he lives with the child.

Parents Share Child-Care

> *When I want to go out and do things, who will watch*
> *the baby? When Jeremiah goes out with his friends, he*
> *wants me to watch the baby. I tell him both of us had the*
> *baby and we share this. So we worked it out so we take*
> *turns. He's real good about it.*

Candi

At least as important to the child is the father's emotional
support. A 16-year-old father, whether or not he lives with his
child's mother, or even if the couple is no longer together at all,
can spend time with his child. He and the mother can negotiate a
sharing of the parental role that will benefit their child. Doing so
is important to the father and mother, and especially to the child.

> *Child-care—that's pretty even. I like taking care of the*
> *kids. I take them across to the playground. When I get off*
> *work, I be tired, and I don't always feel like it. If I don't*
> *take them over there, I'll play with them in the house. They*
> *meet me at the door. That's a nice feeling.*

Jeremiah

> *Who gets up when the baby is screaming? That's one*
> *thing we had to get over—who did what and how. I didn't*
> *used to like the way Maurice changed diapers, but I had to*
> *realize that if he don't practice, he'll never learn.*

Mitzuko, 16/Maurice, 20 (Lana, 14 months)

A high percentage of teens, male and female, were aware in
1984 of the importance of both parents being involved in child-
care tasks. Responses to 1984 and 1994 questions in this area
were similar, most often within three or four percentage points of
each other, for the following tasks: changing baby's diaper,
feeding babies and children, putting baby to bed, disciplining
children, and playing with children (figures 10.5, 10.6).

As the graphs illustrate, the Single females have the *highest*

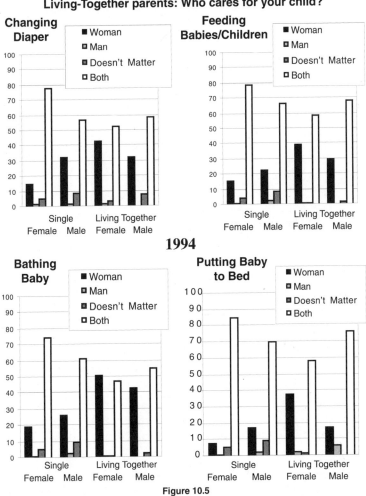

Singles: Who should care for the children?
Living-Together parents: Who cares for your child?

Figure 10.5

expectations of sharing child-care tasks, and the Living-Together females have the *lowest* percentage finding child-care tasks actually shared by partners.

Expectations and realities of the males are not nearly as far apart. In fact, the realities as seen by the fathers show *more* involvement in some areas for those fathers than was expected by the Single males.

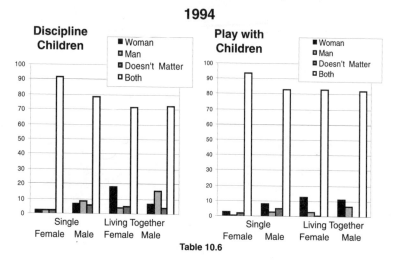

Singles: Who should care for the children?
Living-Together parents: Who cares for your child?

1994

Table 10.6

Summary and Conclusions

A surprisingly low percentage of parents in the survey said their child had a negative effect on their relationship with the other parent. One in five of those not living with a partner felt this way. In the Living-Together group, one in ten females and one in four males reported the relationship deteriorating after their child was born.

About half the young fathers in the survey who live with a partner don't live with their child. Most of them, however, have frequent contact with their child. Of the fathers who don't live with a partner, about two-thirds spend time with their child at least occasionally, and one in four has daily contact.

The majority of fathers from both groups said they would prefer more involvement with their child. Young mothers also would like their children to be more involved with their fathers.

The majority of teen fathers represented in this survey, whether personally or through their child's mother, provide some financial support for their child. These results contradict the stereotype of teen fathers who want nothing to do with either their children or their children's mother.

A majority of Single teens believe that both parents should be responsible for such child-care tasks as diaper changing, feeding babies and toddlers, bathing babies, and disciplining their children. Reality for the Living-Together teens is quite different with mom doing more of the child-care tasks than was expected by the Singles group. Playing with the child is the activity most often shared by both parents.

The author assumes that each partner in a marriage or living-together relationship has equal responsibility for any children they may have, and for supporting themselves. However, mothers in our culture are still likely to take more responsibility for child rearing than do fathers. Society still expects men to take the lead in financially supporting their families—although in many families, both partners must work to maintain themselves and their children.

The reality is that both fathers and mothers need to develop expertise in parenting just as both must learn job skills and prepare for a career.

Knowing how to parent is not instinctual to fathers or mothers. Parenting education is important to both sexes and should be available to all young people. The school with an infant and toddler center on campus can provide a marvelous laboratory for helping young people, those who are already parents *and* those who are not, learn the art and skills of parenting.

Other opportunities for young people to learn parenting skills include GRADS (Graduation, Reality, and Dual-Role Skills) and other school programs for teen parents. Off-campus parenting classes are available in many communities, some of them especially for teenage parents.

A young mother who understands her child's need for a father is likely to encourage the father to be involved. The young man who knows something about parenting is more likely to be involved with his child.

Most young people feel both parents should be involved in caring for their children. Young parents need help in reaching this goal.

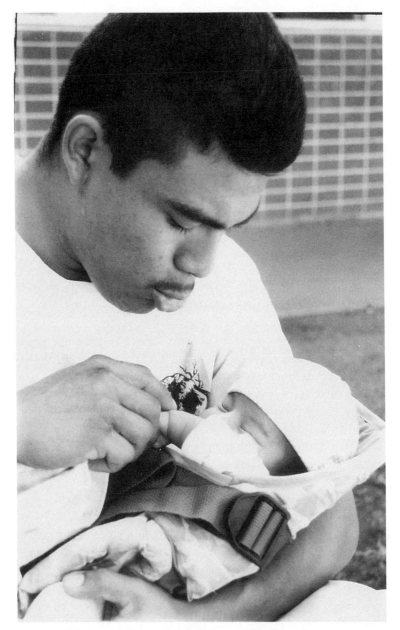

The rate of absentee fathers continues to rise —
yet we know children do better if dad's around along with mom.

CHAPTER 11

Expectations and Reality— Helping Teens Learn to Cope

Both the expectations and the realities of teens have changed considerably in the past decade. So have their perceptions of the way things ought to be.

Following is a review of the high points of the preceding chapters.

Searching for Love — But Not for Marriage

Less than a quarter of today's teens, according to this survey, believe that having sexual intercourse before marriage is wrong. Even fewer are opposed to a couple living together before they marry.

Very few, one in eight teenage women and one in four teenage men, believe a teenage couple should marry if they become pregnant. However, most of these teenagers, men and women, say the man should share responsibility for any pregnancy he causes and for his child.

There were 876 parents in the survey. Three hundred eighty-one were living with a partner, but only 22 percent were married to their child's other parent.

Some of the Living-Together teens who are not married explained their reasons for moving in together without getting married. Many appear to believe strongly that it would not be *right* to marry too soon. Marriage, they say, should be permanent, and they realize they are not ready for that commitment.

Comment: Couples who live together, whether or not they are married, tend to get pregnant and have babies. This value system does not seem to consider strongly enough the pregnancy factor.

This issue will be further discussed later in this chapter.

Change Happens — Can We Cope?

Reinforcing their beliefs that marriage means forever and they are not ready for that commitment, one-quarter of the females and one-third of the males saw negative changes occurring in their partners after they started living together. An even higher percentage (females, 41 percent; males, 35 percent) said living together is harder than they had expected.

About one-quarter of the men and one-third of the women found they had fewer friends after moving in together, and about half said there was less partying.

Suggestion: Single teens might gain some sense of reality through open discussion with teen couples already living together. A panel of couples willing to share openly and honestly can have a strong impact on a class or other discussion group.

Faith and Ethnicity — Must Partners Match?

Nearly half of all respondents, when asked if they would prefer to marry within their own ethnic group, replied, "It doesn't matter." About 42 percent would prefer to marry a person within their own faith. The others don't think this matters either.

About one-third, however, feel that marrying outside one's ethnic group would cause problems, and slightly fewer are concerned about problems if they marry outside their faith.

Almost half the women and two-thirds of the men replied, "Not important" when asked, "How important is religion in your relationship?"

Comment: The difficulty, of course, is that young people change rapidly. Even if a couple feels now that religion is not important to their relationship, one or the other may have quite a different viewpoint later. Couples who start out with similar values tend to have a better chance at succeeding in their relationship.

Traditional Roles No Longer the Norm

A majority of all the young people not yet living with a partner think both partners should share such home management tasks as vacuuming, floor mopping, meal preparation and clean-up, and the family laundry. The 1994 survey showed about a 20 percent increase from 1984 in the proportion expecting partners to share these tasks.

The realities are quite different. Fewer young people living together reported both parents were actually sharing these home management tasks. In fact, the *realities* of 1994 were close to the *expectations* of 1984. In turn, the realities of 1984 showed still fewer partners sharing tasks. Expectations of role-sharing are ahead of the realities, but the realities, too, are changing.

Some of the Living-Together respondents did not feel their partners were as adept as they would like in such areas as cooking, housekeeping, plumbing and other repairs, and yard work. Their evaluation of their partners fell behind the Singles' expectations in these areas.

Suggestion: If one partner expects the couple to share household tasks while the other, most often the man, expects the woman to do most of this work, daily disagreements as to who does what can grow into insurmountable problems. Couples who disagree need to learn how to work through arguments constructively and how to negotiate change. These are skills that can be learned, skills that should be an important part of every relationship or marriage and family living course.

Very young couples who move in together are likely not to

have had a lot of experience in the practicalities of living. Each needs to be encouraged to become as adept as possible at these tasks, and to be patient with the partner's efforts. Taking classes in these areas together would be a positive step, whether in high school or through adult education.

Jealousy — Love's Opponent

Extreme jealousy can destroy a relationship. Many of these teenagers, both those living with a partner and whose who were not, display a great deal of jealousy. The majority would be jealous if their partner "looked" at a member of the opposite sex, and one-fourth had the same feelings if the partner talked with members of the other sex. Even school attendance and working with people of the opposite sex cause problems for about one in five of these young people.

Comment: As women move closer and closer to equality in our society, and at the same time, men retain or regain a similarly equal position, jealousy may be less prevalent. Or to be a little less global and more personal, teens, male and female, who have high self-esteem are likely to have fewer problems with jealousy. Adults who help teens grow into productive human beings are an important part of the solution to the low self-esteem of many youth.

Partner Abuse — Killer of Love

Teen relationships far too often include partner abuse. About one-third of the Living-Together women and even more, two in five, of the Single women, reported having been hit one or more times by a date or partner.

Acceptance of abuse is disturbingly high. From 11 to 21 percent of these respondents said it was either okay for a man to hit his partner, is sometimes necessary, or may happen when he's angry or drunk.

Of the young people I interviewed in 1994, 54 were women. Eighteen of these women reported having been physically abused by their partners, most of them numerous times. Some were no longer with the abusive partner, but others had remained together in spite of the abuse.

Comment: Adults working with teens need to understand how often violence is a factor in teen relationships and do everything possible to help young people understand that no one deserves to be hit. Ideally, such teaching begins long before adolescents enter into partner relationships. Helping our youth avoid violence in their relationships with each other and in other areas of their lives is one of our most important missions.

Your Parents or Mine? Living with In-Laws

Most young couples who live together would prefer to have a home of their own. The majority of teen couples, however, cannot afford that luxury, so many continue to live with his parents or hers.

Lack of privacy, too much supervision, interference in child-rearing, and adjusting to quite different life styles are problems frequently encountered by young people in this situation.

Having a good relationship with one's own parents would seem to be an advantage in adjusting to life with one's partner's family. However, young people in the survey who already live with a partner were less likely to have spent their growing-up years with their father, and, to a lesser extent, with their mother. Fewer of the Living-Together teens, as compared to the Singles, reported a good relationship with either mother or father. These factors may account for some teens' decisions to move in with the partner's family. The moving may be at least partly seen as an opportunity to leave a family situation considered by the teen to be negative.

Suggestion: Encouraging young people to understand the many different ways people live may help prepare them for extended family living. Communication skills can aid in problem-solving. Thorough planning and agreeing, if possible, on each person's responsibilities *ahead* of the move-in can prevent some of the problems.

A couple who adjusts well to a period of extended family living and learns to appreciate the ways of both families may find they have made a positive start toward a long-term and satisfying relationship with each other.

On Dropping Out and Moving In

A quarter of the Living-Together respondents said their school attendance worsened or they dropped out of school after moving in with a partner. More than a third of the young women in the survey said their partners had actually dropped out of school.

Many of these young couples already had a child. Many of the young women spoke of partners who wanted them to drop out of school, partners who appeared threatened by the young woman's interest in education and job training.

Comment: Both parents need to graduate from high school and go on to further education and/or job training in order to be able to support their families adequately. The dropout rate in many of our schools, as exemplified in these statistics, is a sad reflection on the value our culture places on education.

Suggestion: Adults who work with young people, and especially with young parents, can make a real difference by providing inviting opportunities for learning and for developing job skills and positive attitudes toward work. Too often today the funding for such programs is being cut—a tragedy for young people and for our society.

Men Who Don't Work and Women Who Do

Traditional marriage, in which the man earns the money and the woman stays home, has almost ceased to exist, according to these young people.

The vast majority of these young men and women expect to work. Only when their children are under two years of age do even a third of the women expect to stay home (although about half of their partners suggest the woman not work during this time). The percentage of women planning to work shoots up to 86 percent when the children are aged 2-5, and 94-96 percent after that. Considerably fewer, but still a healthy majority, of the men expect their partners to work during these years.

If they have no children or the children are in school, a
smaller percentage of men than women expect to work away
from home. Even when the children are aged 2-5, Living-
Together males are slightly less likely, as compared to females,
to expect to have jobs. Only when the children are younger than
two are the men more likely than the women to expect to work
away from home.

Suggestion: As indicated in chapter 9, this shift in job expectations means we must no longer concentrate on job skills for
men and home management and child-rearing skills for women.
Both partners must be able and willing to share both roles.

Career education must be designed to enable young people to
be job-ready and to find jobs that will provide both money and
work satisfaction. We need to help young people understand the
joys of providing financially for one's family and in parenting
well.

Quality, available child-care is an important ingredient in
meeting this goal. Child-care for the children of teenage parents
can make the difference between parents who must rely on
welfare for support and those who don't. Parents who must drop
out of school because of no child-care often have no alternative
except to rely on welfare. Parents who are able to continue their
education while their children receive quality care, on the other
hand, are far more likely to become working, tax-paying adults.

Providing child-care on high school campuses is actually cost-
effective when one considers the additional earning power of
parents able to finish school.

"He's My Baby, Too"—Teen Dads *Are* Involved

About one in six of the Single parent respondents felt their
child had had a negative effect on their relationship with the
other parent. Surprisingly, few mothers in the Living-Together
survey felt this way. Of the Living-Together group, only one in
ten of the females, but one in *four* of the males said their
relationship had deteriorated after their child was born.

Although about half the fathers in the Living-Together group
don't live with their child and the child's mother, most of them

have frequent contact with the child. About two-thirds of the fathers in the Singles group say they spend time with their child at least occasionally, and one in four has daily contact. The majority of the fathers and mothers in both groups would like the fathers to see their children more often.

The majority of the teen fathers represented in the survey provide some financial support for their child.

A majority of the Single teens believe both parents should be responsible for child-care tasks, while a smaller percentage of the Living-Together parents say this is the reality in their homes.

Comment: Fathers and mothers need to share in the child rearing and the financial support in their families. *Both* parents are needed by their children.

Suggestion: It is equally important to teach young men and young women parenting skills, job skills, and career development.

Teen Parents — Equality for Dad, Equality for Mom

Of the 97 fathers in the survey, only 36 live with their children while almost all of the mothers and children are together. Of all the teenage respondents, from 43 to 58 percent had lived less than ten years with their fathers. Only one in ten had lived less than ten years with their mothers. The pattern of dad's absence continues.

A lot of people are doing a lot of tongue-clucking about absent fathers. Research shows that, surprise, surprise, children do better if dad's around along with mom. Yet the rate of absentee fathers continues to rise.

We know that dad is important. But do we really believe he's as important a parent as mom?

Recently I observed a young mother carrying a child, perhaps 15 months old. The mother was lovely, and the child, looking over her mother's shoulder, was beautiful. Suddenly, in my mind, the mother became the father, and the picture of parent and child was every bit as beautiful and as touching. But do we *really* believe fathers are as important as mothers?

It occurred to me that we often don't give men the chance truly to succeed as a fully nurturing parent. As a starter, if the parents are not together, it is generally assumed that the mother will be the custodial parent, especially if the couple has never been married.

The pattern of mom being in charge and dad only a helper, however, is also typical of parents who intend to parent together. Often, before their baby is born, mom has had more child-care experience than dad. She already knows how to change the baby. She probably has learned how to soothe an infant. Dad may not have had this pre-baby experience, and from the beginning, he feels like the helper rather than a full partner in parenting. Perhaps this can work fairly well in families where dad earns the money and mom takes care of the children and the house. Each has an important job to do. Each can get tremendous satisfaction from knowing s/he plays a vital role in the family.

But the world has changed. No longer, as indicated above, is dad the sole breadwinner. Mom, too, probably has a job, and her paycheck along with his is required to keep the family fed and housed. At the same time, in many families, mom is still doing far more than her share in the child-care and home management areas.

If a parent needs to take the child to the doctor, most often it is mom who must get off work or miss school to do so. She is likely to be the one who organizes the child-care. Sometimes, the father who spends an evening with his child is even called the *baby-sitter.* (The dictionary defines baby-sitting as caring for children during the *absence* of their parents.)

Usually we look at this situation, and we say it isn't fair to mom. She has far too much responsibility and too much to do. And that's often true.

However, there is another way to see this reality. Dad is no longer the primary wage earner. He often has not had much experience in child-care and home management. His partner is much more efficient at these tasks. Besides, he has grown up thinking it's her job and that she does, indeed, know much more about these things than he does.

The resulting feelings for a man may well be that he doesn't "own" any part of the family responsibilities any more. He can't earn enough money to support the family by himself, so his partner has to work, too. Sometimes, in fact, she will have a better job and earn more money than he does. At the same time, he doesn't feel—or act—"in charge" at home.

Could this be part of the reality behind those 11-25 percent of young men who don't plan to work while they have small children? (See chapter 9.) They no longer can expect, even if they want to, to be in charge of the money-earning role. At the same time, they are definitely second in the child-care hierarchy. So what is their role?

This does not make it right for young men to forego financial responsibility, nor does it make it right for young men not to do their share of the work of child-rearing and home management. It doesn't make it right, but it may help us understand these realities a little better.

With that understanding, perhaps we can do a better job of helping young men, even as we help young women, understand that both men and women often must shoulder together the financial support of their families. At the same time, we must help young men *better understand their importance in the parenting and homemaking arena.* Only then can we expect men to understand and buy into the reality of dual-role couples, and the joys of a truly sharing partnership.

We have a long way to go in finding full equality for women in our culture, but as we make ever stronger efforts to do so, let's don't throw the men out with the bath water. Let's help men understand their children need them every bit as much as those children need their mothers. We still need women *and* men in our families.

Teaching Responsible Sexuality

In these chapters, we have looked at teenagers' expectations of and attitudes toward living together. We have studied the realities in the lives of teens already married or living together.

Many of the problems faced by these young couples are obvious. Solutions are not.

The recommendations made so far deal mostly with relationship-building skills and the need for improving the quality of education for young men and young women. These recommendations are important if we are to deal with the problems discussed in these chapters.

Even more basic than the need for a good education, however, is the problem of too-early parenthood. In chapter 1, the majority of teens' acceptance of intercourse before marriage, living together before marriage, and not marrying too early combined with our society's bias against adequate sex education for our youth equals babies born to parents not yet ready to shoulder together the responsibilities of parenting. Lots of babies, about half a million, are born each year to teenage mothers in the United States. From one-fourth to one-third of the fathers of these babies are also teenagers.

Abstaining from sexual intercourse until marriage is a fine practice, and young people need lots of support for that decision. But that support is not enough. We absolutely must understand that adolescents are indeed part of our society. They see the sexy ads and the movies and television with explicit sex scenes. They hear the music urging them over and over to "do it." And the majority are "doing it" by age 18.

What they don't hear often enough is the message of *responsible* sex. Birth control generally isn't part of the sex scene in the media. Sadly, neither is birth control part of the education offered in many school districts across our country. Too often, when sex education is provided, students get a week or two of plumbing information. And people wonder why teens are having babies!

As a society, we could prevent some of the tragedies resulting from too-early marriage/living together and from unplanned pregnancy. First, family life education should be provided for all students from kindergarten through high school. As young people mature, they need to understand the responsibilities involved in being a sexually developing human being.

The premise behind the lack of sex education in many areas is the idea that young people will become more sexually active if they are offered sex education classes. However, studies show that sex education does *not* increase sexual activity among the young people involved, but that it does cut down on the number of pregnancies experienced by these young people.

Delaying sexual activity until adulthood is a sensible aim, and abstinence must be an acceptable choice for teenagers. It is not realistic, however, to concentrate on abstinence as the complete answer. Teenagers are greatly affected by our culture's preoccupation with sex as seen in movies, on TV, in advertisements, and throughout the media, and abstinence is *not* the media's message.

Contraception alone will not solve the problem of adolescent pregnancy. Certainly some teenagers would continue to become pregnant even if contraceptives were free and readily available to everyone. But contraception *is* part of the solution, an important part. When access to contraception is limited for teenagers, the result is more pregnancies, not less sexual activity. Some high schools in the United States provide on-campus health services which include the dispensing of contraceptives, surely a rational approach to the realities of teenage sexual activity.

We expect young people to be responsible in their attitudes and actions in the area of sex. Not including this topic in a school's curriculum does not seem to be a responsible approach on the part of the school or the community. Schools have a responsibility to their communities to help young people become responsible citizens. Practical sex education should be an integral part of that responsibility.

Help for Pregnant and Parenting Teens

In addition, all secondary schools need to offer special services for pregnant students and teenage parents. These young people too often drop out of school only to become dependent on our social service system. School programs with good outreach as a component can make a difference in these young people's lives—and result in reduced expense to taxpayers.

The babies born to teenage mothers are the winners when their mothers and fathers are able to continue school, get good jobs, and feel good about themselves. Some schools offer special classes for pregnant students. Some provide infant care on campus so that after the baby is born, the young parents can continue attending school and, at the same time, learn parenting skills.

The need for child-care for the children of school-age parents is basic. Good infant care is expensive, but more expensive to society and to taxpayers are the young parents who must rely on welfare for support because they dropped out of school and are unable to get and keep good jobs. The high cost of child-care on campus for students' babies is more than offset by the contributions most of these young people will make as they become productive members of our society.

Side effects of the provision of child-care services in schools are the benefits to the babies. In a top-notch center, young parents learn the parenting skills they need in order to help their babies develop to their fullest potential. If young parents receive the help they need during the child's all-important first years, their child may be better able to cope with school, with jobs, with life than his/her parents are.

Summary and Conclusions

Even though most teenagers no longer feel pregnancy is a reason to get married, moving in with the partner often follows teenage pregnancy. If the relationship fails, the child is likely to suffer at least as much, often more than the parents do.

Adolescence, pregnancy, and living together are a triple dilemma for the young people involved, and for their families. If the woman becomes pregnant early in the relationship, she is likely to feel dependent at the same time the young man is feeling the stress of more responsibility than he expected at this point in his life. Seemingly insurmountable difficulties may wreck the relationship.

To overcome these problems, each partner needs to form a strong individual identity while the couple works together to develop a committed and intimate relationship. Even if they succeed in coping with the demands of living together, and perhaps the demands of parenthood, they still must face some basic issues. Completing their education, then finding and keeping satisfying, adequately-paid jobs while dealing with the demands of daily living will undoubtedly be a challenge to the young couple.

Most people in the United States marry at some time during their lives. Young people in the survey want, when they do marry, a lifetime commitment.

If a young couple decides to marry or to live together, their chances of coping will be increased if each has a good sense of self-worth. They are likely to have less difficulty with communication, jealousy, sex, and other relationship problems.

Building self-esteem is a life-long process. From infancy to adulthood and throughout life, people need to value themselves. Parents and schools play an integral role in the task of helping young people develop positive self-esteem. This is without a doubt one of the most important tasks of parenting and of teaching.

If a young person has good self-esteem, s/he will be more likely to be able to make wise decisions in all areas of life. Delaying marriage and parenthood until after adolescent development is completed gives young people more choices and generally a better chance at a satisfying life. They are less likely to settle into low-paying jobs with little chance of advancement. Those who delay marriage and/or moving in with a partner until they are adults are more likely to develop a long-lasting and caring relationship and to provide a better life for their children.

Teenage Couples—Expectations and Reality has presented a picture of teenagers' attitudes toward marriage and living together, and of some of the realities faced by teenage couples. The culture of these young people is a mixture of adolescent dependence and adult responsibility. Combining the two roles is never easy.

The rainbows, roles and realities of teenage partnerships are many-faceted. Some young couples, with much trust, respect, and caring, will be able to develop a satisfying long-term relationship. They are to be commended.

APPENDIX

Single Teens' Expectations of Marriage and/or Living Together

We'd like your opinions about marriage and living together. We'll use this in a book on this subject.

If you are *not* married and have never lived with a partner, please take the questionnaire on WHITE paper. If you *are* married or have ever lived with a partner, please be sure you have the YELLOW questionnaire.

- Please do *not* put your name or other identifying data on your questionnaire or answer sheet. Instead, please write "**WHITE**" (the color of your questionnaire) in the name space.

- Remember—opinions are not right or wrong. They are simply opinions. Please be honest and open as you answer these questions. Your opinions are important!

- Use a black lead pencil to fill in appropriate circles on your answer sheet. Make heavy black marks that fill in the circle completely.

- Erase cleanly any answer you wish to change. Make no stray marks on your answer sheet.

- In a few questions, you are told that more than one answer is okay. On all of the other questions, please choose the *one* answer closest to what you think. If the question does not apply to you, leave the answer section blank.

- If you would like to comment on any of the questions, please do so. Write on a separate sheet of paper. Then clip this paper to your answer sheet. Thank you.

1. Are you married or have you ever lived with a partner?
   A. No   B. Yes   C. We lived together but live separately now.

If your answer to the above question was "No," (A), your entire questionnaire should be on WHITE paper.

If your answer to this question was B or C, your questionnaire should be on YELLOW paper.

IF YOU HAVE THE WRONG COLOR QUESTIONNAIRE, PLEASE ASK YOUR TEACHER FOR THE CORRECT ONE. (The color you write on your answer sheet *must* match the color of your questionnaire.)

2. How old are you?
   A. 12 or younger   B. 13   C. 14   D. 15   E. 16
   F. 17   G. 18   H. 19   I. 20 or older

3. Your sex: A. Male   B. Female

4. Highest level of education that you have completed:
   A. 6 B. 7 C. 8 D. 9 E. 10 F. 11 G. High school grad
   H. Some college or post high school training program

5. Kind of school you attend:
   A. High school or junior high
   B. Special school for pregnant and/or parenting teens
   C. Continuation or other alternative school
   D. Trade or vocational school   E. Private school
   F. Not in school   G. Other

6. Where do you live?
   A. City   B. Suburb   C. Rural area

7. To which ethnic group do you feel you belong?
   A. Anglo   B. Hispanic   C. Asian   D. African American
   E. Native American   F. Mixed

8. Your religious group:
   A. Catholic   B. Protestant   C. Born-Again Christian
   D. Jewish   E. Muslim   F. Other   G. No religious affiliation

9. Your marital status:
   A. Single   B. Engaged   C. Living together, but not married
   D. Married   E. Separated   F. Divorced   G. Widowed

10. Highest school grade or degree completed by your mother:
    A. Grade 8   B. Grade 9   C. Grade 10   D. Grade 11
    E. Grade 12   F. Some college   G. 2-year college degree
    H. 4-year college degree   I. Advanced degree   J. I don't know

11. Highest school grade or degree completed by your father:
    A. Grade 8   B. Grade 9   C. Grade 10   D. Grade 11
    E. Grade 12   F. Some college   G. 2-year college degree
    H. 4-year college degree   I. Advanced degree   J. I don't know

12. For how long have you lived with your father?
    A. Never   B. Birth to 2 years   C. 3-5 years
    D. 6-10 years   E. Eleven years or more   F. All my life

13. For how long have you lived with your mother?
    A. Never   B. Birth to 2 years   C. 3-5 years
    D. 6-10 years   E. Eleven years or more   F. All my life

14. Is your relationship with your mother
    A. Excellent   B. Good   C. Fair   D. Poor   E. No relationship

15. Is your relationship with your father
    A. Excellent   B. Good   C. Fair   D. Poor   E. No relationship

16. With whom do you now live? (Mark all that apply to you.)
    A. Mother   B. Father   C. Other relative(s)   D. Foster parent(s)
    E. Live alone   F. Husband/wife   G. Boy/girlfriend
    H. Partner's family   I. Friends   J. Other

17. How do you feel about a young couple living with his or her parents?
    A. Good idea   B. Okay until we save some money
    C. I would rather not   D. I'm totally against it

18. Is it all right for a couple to have sexual intercourse before they marry?
    A. Absolutely   B. Probably   C. It doesn't matter
    D. Probably not   E. Absolutely not

19. How do you feel about a man and woman living together if they aren't married?
    A. It's okay   B. It's okay *if* they plan to marry later
    C. It's okay but I wouldn't do it   D. I think it's wrong

20. When a teenage girl gets pregnant, should she and her boyfriend marry?
    A. Absolutely   B. Probably   C. It depends on their situation
    D. Probably not   E. Absolutely not

21. Do you think it's important for a child to live with both of his/her parents?
    A. Absolutely   B. Probably   C. I don't know
    D. Probably not   E. Absolutely not

22. **FOR FEMALES:** Are you now or have you ever been pregnant?
    (Mark each answer that applies to you.)
    A. I have never been pregnant.   B. I'm pregnant now.
    C. I was pregnant, but I miscarried.
    D. I was pregnant, but I had an abortion.
    E. I had a baby that I placed for adoption.
    F. I have one or more children now.

    FOR MALES: Have you ever gotten a girl pregnant?
    A. No.   B. Yes, one girl.
    C. Yes, more than one girl.   D. I don't know.

23. If a man gets a woman pregnant, should he take responsibility for the pregnancy and the child?
    A. Absolutely   B. Probably   C. I don't know
    D. Probably not   E. Absolutely not

24. **FOR MALES AND FEMALES:** Do you already have one or more children? How many?
    A. No   B. Yes—one   C. Yes—two
    D. Yes —three   E. Yes—four or more

If you answered No to the above question, please skip to question #33 If you have a child, please answer #25-32.

25. If you have one or more children, please mark the age of each:
    A. Under 6 months B. 6-11 months   C. 12-17 months
    D. 18-23 months   E. 24-29 months F. 30-35 months   G. 3 years

26. Are you married to your child's other parent?
    A. Yes   B. No   C. We were, but separated   D. We are divorced

27. Who has legal custody of your child?
    A. Mother *and* father   B. Child's mother
    C. Child's father   D. Grandparent(s)   E. Other

28. Who is mostly responsible for your child's care?
    FEMALES:
    A. I am   B. The child's father   C. My parent(s)
    D. Baby's father's parent(s)   E. Another relative
    F. Friend   G. Baby-sitter   H. Other.

    MALES:
    A. I am   B. The child's mother   C. My parent(s)
    D. Baby's mother's parent(s)   E. Another relative
    F. Friend   G. Baby-sitter   H. Other

29. **FOR MALES:** How involved are you in your child's life?
    A. I am not involved with my child at all.
    B. I see my child only occasionally.
    C. My child lives elsewhere, and I see him once or twice a month.
    D. My child lives elsewhere and I see him at least once a week.
    E. My child lives elsewhere but I see him daily.
    F. I live with my child and his/her mother.
    G. I have sole custody of my child.

    FOR FEMALES: Is the father involved in your child's life?
    A. He is not involved with my child.
    B. He sees our child only occasionally.
    C. He sees our child once or twice a month.
    D. He sees our child at least once a week.
    E. He lives elsewhere, but sees our child daily.
    F. He lives with our child and me.
    G. He has sole custody of our child.

30. **FOR MALES:** Do you provide financial support for your child?
    A. I pay no child support at this time.
    B. I give my child's mother money occasionally to buy things for my
       child.
    C. I pay a fixed amount of child support each month.
    D. I provide complete financial support for my child.

    FOR FEMALES: Does your child's father provide any financial support
    for your child?
    A. The father pays no child support.
    B. The father occasionally pays for diapers and other things for our child.
    C. The father is paying a fixed amount of child support each month.
    D. The father provides complete financial support for our child.

31. **FOR MALES:** Would you like to be more involved with your child?
    A. Yes   B. Possibly   C. No   D. I don't want to be involved at all.

    FOR FEMALES: Would you like your child's father to be more involved with your child?
    A. Yes   B. Possibly   C. No   D. I don't want him involved at all.

32. What effect has your child had on your relationship with his/her other parent?
    A. Very good   B. Somewhat good   C. No effect
    D. Somewhat bad   E. Very bad

33. If you have a problem, to whom are you most likely to talk? **(Please be sure to put answer on row #33.)**
    A. Nobody   B. Parents   C. Boy/girlfriend (or husband/wife)
    D. Another friend E. Teacher   F. Counselor
    G. Minister   H. Other

34. When you and your boyfriend/girlfriend have an argument, how do you settle it? (More than one answer is okay.)
    A. Quit talking to each other.   B. Yell to get rid of bad feelings.
    C. Talk it through together.   D. Talk to my parents or hers.
    E. Talk to someone else.   F. Slug it out.
    G. Get a referee.   H. We do not argue.

35. How do you feel about a man hitting his partner?
    A. It should never happen.
    B. It's not good, but sometimes it's necessary.
    C. It's not okay, but it may happen when he's angry or drunk.
    D. It's okay.

36. How do you feel about a woman hitting her partner?
    A. It should never happen.
    B. It's not good, but sometimes it's necessary.
    C. It's not okay, but it may happen when he's angry or drunk.
    D. It's okay.

37. Has a date or your partner ever hit you?
    A. Never   B. Once   C. Two times
    D. Three times E. Four times F. Five or more

38. Have you ever hit a date or your partner?
    A. Never   B. Once   C. Two times
    D. Three times E. Four times F. Five or more

39. Would you prefer to marry a person from your own ethnic group or race?
    A. Absolutely   B. Probably   C. It doesn't matter
    D. Probably not   E. Absolutely not

40. Do you think marrying a person from a different ethnic group would cause problems for you?
    A. Absolutely   B. Probably   C. I don't know
    D. Probably not   E. Absolutely not

41. Would you prefer to marry a person who has the same religious beliefs as you do?
    A. Absolutely   B. Probably   C. It doesn't matter
    D. Probably not   E. Absolutely not

42. Do you think marrying a person with different religious beliefs would cause problems for you?
    A. Absolutely   B. Probably   C. I don't know
    D. Probably not   E. Absolutely not

43. When/if you marry, would you like your marriage to be much like your parents' marriage?
    A. Absolutely   B. Probably   C. It doesn't matter
    D. Probably not   E. Absolutely not

44. When you get married, do you expect it to last the rest of your life?
    A. Absolutely   B. Probably   C. It doesn't matter
    D. Probably not   E. Absolutely not

How much do you think getting married or living with a partner at age 18 or younger would change your life in the following areas?

45. **Money:**   A. I'd have more money
    B. It would make no difference   C. I'd have less money

46. **Friends:**   A. More friends   B. Fewer friends
    C. Different friends   D. No change

47. **Recreation/Partying:**   A. More   B. No change   C. Less

48. **Free Time:**   A. More   B. No change   C. Less

49. **Relationship with your family:**
    A. Closer   B. No change   C. Less close

50. **School attendance:** A. Attendance would improve   B.   No change
    C. Attendance would drop   D. I would drop out of school

51. **College/Trade school:**   A. I'd be more likely to attend
    B. No change   C. Less likely to attend

52. If you married or moved in with a partner before you graduated from high
    school, would you want your partner to continue his/her education?
    A. Absolutely   B. Probably   C. It doesn't matter
    D. Probably not   E. Absolutely not

53. For your marriage to be successful, would you and your partner need to
    have enough money for your important needs?
    A. Absolutely   B. Probably   C. It doesn't matter
    D. Probably not   E. Absolutely not

54. Should married or living-together partners agree on how they spend
    money?
    A. Absolutely   B. Probably   C. It doesn't matter
    D. Probably not   E. Absolutely not

55. In a *good* marriage, should the husband earn most of the money?
    A. Absolutely   B. Probably   C. It doesn't matter
    D. Probably not   E. Absolutely not

56. In a *good* marriage, should the wife do most of the cooking and
    housekeeping?
    A. Absolutely   B. Probably   C. It doesn't matter
    D. Probably not   E. Absolutely not

57. Do you think it is important for a mother and father to agree on how to
    discipline their children?
    A. Absolutely   B. Probably   C. It doesn't matter
    D. Probably not   E. Absolutely not

**If/when you marry or live with a partner, who do you feel should be
responsible for the following tasks?**

58. **Earning money:**   A. Woman only   B. Woman mostly
    C. Both   D. Man mostly   E. Man only   F. Doesn't matter

59. **Deciding how money is spent:** A. Woman only   B. Woman mostly
    C. Both   D. Man mostly   E. Man only   F. Doesn't matter

60. **Paying bills:**   A. Woman only   B. Woman mostly
    C. Both   D. Man mostly   E. Man only   F. Doesn't matter

61. **Vacuuming the house:**   A. Woman only   B. Woman mostly
    C. Both   D. Man mostly   E. Man only   F. Doesn't matter

62. **Mopping floors:**   A. Woman only   B. Woman mostly
    C. Both   D. Man mostly   E. Man only   F. Doesn't matter

63. **Preparing meals:**   A. Woman only   B. Woman mostly
    C. Both   D. Man mostly   E. Man only   F. Doesn't matter

64. **Cleaning up after meals:** A. Woman only   B. Woman mostly
    C. Both   D. Man mostly   E. Man only   F. Doesn't matter

65. **Doing family laundry:**   A. Woman only   B. Woman mostly
    C. Both   D. Man mostly   E. Man only   F. Doesn't matter

66. **Washing the car:**   A. Woman only   B. Woman mostly
    C. Both   D. Man mostly   E. Man only   F. Doesn't matter

67. **Mowing the lawn:**   A. Woman only   B. Woman mostly
    C. Both   D. Man mostly   E. Man only   F. Doesn't matter

68. **Changing baby's diapers:** A. Woman only   B. Woman mostly
    C. Both   D. Man mostly   E. Man only   F. Doesn't matter

69. **Feeding babies/children:** A. Woman only   B. Woman mostly
    C. Both   D. Man mostly   E. Man only   F. Doesn't matter

70. **Bathing baby:**   A. Woman only   B. Woman mostly
    C. Both   D. Man mostly   E. Man only   F. Doesn't matter

71. **Putting baby to bed:**   A. Woman only   B. Woman mostly
    C. Both   D. Man mostly   E. Man only   F. Doesn't matter

72. **Putting toddler to bed:** A. Woman only   B. Woman mostly
    C. Both   D. Man mostly   E. Man only   F. Doesn't matter

73. **Disciplining children:**   A. Woman only   B. Woman mostly
    C. Both   D. Man mostly   E. Man only   F. Doesn't matter

74. **Playing with the children:** A. Woman only   B. Woman mostly
    C. Both   D. Man mostly   E. Man only   F. Doesn't matter

172

Questionnaire

How important is it that the person you eventually marry/live with have the following qualities?

75. **Good money manager:**
    A. Very important   B. Somewhat important   C. Not important

76. **Loves and cares about children:**
    A. Very important   B. Somewhat important   C. Not important

77. **Good cook:**
    A. Very important   B. Somewhat important   C. Not important

78. **Good housekeeper:**
    A. Very important   B. Somewhat important   C. Not important

79. **Knows how to make plumbing and other home repairs:**
    A. Very important   B. Somewhat important   C. Not important

80. **Takes care of the yard:**
    A. Very important   B. Somewhat important   C. Not important

81. **Good sex partner:**
    A. Very important   B. Somewhat important   C. Not important

82. **Shares common interests with you:**
    A. Very important   B. Somewhat important   C. Not important

83. **Spends most of his/her time with you:**
    A. Very important   B. Somewhat important   C. Not important

84. Do you expect to work outside your home if you have no children?
    A. Yes   B. Probably   C. Probably not   D. Absolutely not

85. Do you expect your partner to work outside your home if you have no children?
    A. Yes   B. Probably   C. Probably not   D. Absolutely not

86. Do you expect to work outside your home if you have children under two years of age?
    A. Yes   B. Probably   C. Probably not   D. Absolutely not

87. Do you expect your partner to work outside your home if you have children under two years of age?
    A. Yes   B. Probably   C. Probably not   D. Absolutely not

88. Do you expect to work outside your home if you have children aged two to five?

    A. Yes   B. Probably   C. Probably not   D. Absolutely not

89. Do you expect your partner to work outside your home if you have children aged two to five?

    A. Yes   B. Probably   C. Probably not   D. Absolutely not

90. Do you expect to work outside your home if all your children are in school?

    A. Yes   B. Probably   C. Probably not   D. Absolutely not

91. Do you expect your partner to work outside your home if all your children are in school?

    A. Yes   B. Probably   C. Probably not   D. Absolutely not

92. Would it be all right with you if the woman in your partnership earned more money than the man?

    A. Yes   B. Probably   C. Probably not   D. Absolutely not

93. Is it all right for a man to tell his partner that she must *not* work away from home?

    A. Yes   B. Probably   C. Probably not   D. Absolutely not

94. Is it all right for a man to tell his partner that she *must* work away from home?

    A. Yes   B. Probably   C. Probably not   D. Absolutely not

95. Is it all right for a man to stay home while his partner gets a job?

    A. Yes   B. Probably   C. Probably not   D. Absolutely not

96. **MALES:** Would you be jealous if your girlfriend or wife looked at other boys?

    FEMALES: Would you be jealous if your boyfriend or husband looked at other girls?

    A. Absolutely   B. Probably   C. I don't know
    D. Probably not   E. Absolutely not

97. **MALES:** Would you be jealous if your girlfriend or wife talked with other boys?

    FEMALES: Would you be jealous if your boyfriend or husband talked with other girls?

    A. Absolutely   B. Probably   C. I don't know
    D. Probably not   E. Absolutely not

98. **MALES:** Would you be jealous if your girlfriend or wife worked with other boys?
    FEMALES: Would you be jealous if your boyfriend or husband worked with other girls?
    A. Absolutely   B. Probably   C. I don't know
    D. Probably not   E. Absolutely not

99. **MALES:** Would you be jealous if your girlfriend or wife went to school with other boys?
    FEMALES: Would you be jealous if your boyfriend or husband went to school with other girls?
    A. Absolutely   B. Probably   C. I don't know
    D. Probably not   E. Absolutely not

100. **MALES:** Would you be jealous if your girlfriend or wife went to a concert with another boy?
     FEMALES: Would you be jealous if your boyfriend or husband went to a concert with another girl?
     A. Absolutely   B. Probably   C. I don't know
     D. Probably not   E. Absolutely not

101. **MALES:** Would you be jealous if your girlfriend or wife had a close male friend?
     FEMALES: Would you be jealous if your boyfriend or husband had a close female friend?
     A. Absolutely   B. Probably   C. I don't know
     D. Probably not   E. Absolutely not

Please add any comments you wish about any of the questions. Write your comments on another sheet of paper, then clip them to your answer sheet.

This is the end of the survey. I plan to send your school a copy of the results of this survey. If you are interested, please check with your teacher — or write to me:

Jeanne Lindsay
6595 San Haroldo Way • Buena Park, CA 90620-3748

THANK YOU VERY MUCH!

Realities
of Living-Together Teens

(**NOTE:** Questions 1-33 are the same as in the preceding questionnaire.)

34. How long have you been married? (If you are separated or divorced, how long were you married?)

    A. Not married   B. 0-3 months   C. 4-6 months
    D. 7-12 months   E. 1-2 years   F. More than two years

35. **FOR FEMALES:** Were you pregnant and/or a parent when you got married and/or started living together? (If more than one answer applies, check both.)

    A. No   B. I was pregnant   C. My partner and I already had a child.
    D. I already had a child by a different man.

    FOR MALES: Was your partner pregnant and/or a parent when you got married and/or started living together? (If more than one answer applies, check each one.)
    A. No   B. She was pregnant   C. We already had a child.
    D. She already had a child by a different man.

36. While living together, have you and your partner lived by yourselves?
    A. Yes, always   B. Yes, part of the time   C. No

37. With whom have the two of you lived? Check more than one if necessary.
    A. *Always* by ourselves   B. His parents   C. Her parents
    D. Other relatives   E. Friends   F. Other

38. Is your partner from your own ethnic group or race?
    A. Yes **(SKIP TO #40)**   B. No   C. Partly

39. If you do not belong to the same ethnic group, how has this affected you?
    A. No problem at all.   B. It's a problem only to our parents.
    C. Sometimes causes problems for us.   D. It's a big problem for us.

40. Do you and your partner have similar religious beliefs? **(Answer in Row #40)**   A. Yes   B. Somewhat   C. No

41. Does either of you belong to a church?
    A. No   B. Yes, one of us   C. Yes, both of us

42. Do you and your partner belong to the same church?
    A. Yes **(Skip to #44)**   B. No

43. How has this affected your relationship?
    A. No problem at all.   B. It's a problem only to our parents.
    C. Occasionally causes problems for us.   D. It's a big problem for us.

44. How important is religion in your relationship? **(Answer in Row #44.)**
    A. Very important   B. Mildly important   C. Not important

45. Is the relationship between you and your partner much like your parents'
    relationship?   A. Yes   B. Somewhat alike   C. Not alike at all

46. Do you and your partner have similar interests?
    A. Yes   B. Somewhat similar   C. No

47. Is a lack of similar interests ever a problem?
    A. Yes   B. Sometimes   C. No

48. Do you and your partner find it easy to talk and share feelings with each
    other?   A. Yes   B. Sometimes   C. No

49. Do you think lack of communication is a problem in your relationship?
    A. Yes   B. Sometimes   C. No

50. If you have a problem, to whom are you most likely to talk?
    A. Nobody   B. Parents   C. Boy/girl friend (or husband/wife)
    D. Another friend   E. Teacher   F. Counselor
    G. Minister   H. Other

51. If you are upset with your partner, what do you do? (More than one answer is okay.)
    A. Tell him/her you are upset.   B. Leave and think it through.
    C. Hit him/her.   D. Tell a friend or parent, but not your partner.
    E. I don't do anything.

52. When you and your boyfriend/girlfriend have an argument, how do you settle it? (More than one answer is okay.)
    A. Quit talking to each other.   B. Yell to get rid of bad feelings.
    C. Talk it through together.   D. Talk to my parents or his/hers.
    E. Talk to someone else.   F. Slug it out.
    G. Get a referee.   H. We do not argue.

53. How do you feel about a man hitting his partner?
    A. It should never happen.
    B. It's not good, but sometimes it's necessary.
    C. It's not okay, but it may happen when he's angry or drunk.
    D. It's okay.

54. How do you feel about a woman hitting her partner?
    A. It should never happen.
    B. It's not good, but sometimes it's necessary.
    C. It's not okay, but it may happen when she's angry or drunk.
    D. It's okay.

55. Has your partner ever hit you?   A. Never   B. Once
    C. Two times   D. Three times   E. Four times   F. Five or more

56. Have you ever hit your partner?   A. Never   B. Once
    C. Two times   D. Three times   E. Four times   F. Five or more

57. Has your partner changed much since you were married or started living together?   A. Much positive change   B. Some positive change
    C. No change   D. Some negative change   E. Much negative change

58. Compared to what you expected before you started living together, living together is: A. Easier   B. About what I expected   C. Harder

59. Is sex an important part of your relationship?
    A. Absolutely   B. Somewhat important   C. It doesn't matter
    D. Not especially   E. Absolutely not

60. Are you happy with your partnership?
    A. Yes   B. Most of the time, yes   C. Sometimes
    D. Most of the time, no   E. No

61. Do you expect your current relationship to last the rest of your life?
    A. Absolutely   B. Probably   C. It doesn't matter
    D. Probably not   E. Absolutely not

How much has getting married or living with your partner changed your life in the following areas?

62. **Money:**   A. I have more money   B. It has made no difference
    C. I have less money

63. **Friends:**   A. More friends   B. Fewer friends
    C. Different friends   D. No change

64. **Recreation/Partying:**   A. More
    B. No change   C. Less

65. **Free Time:**   A. More   B. No change   C. Less

66. **Relationship with your family:**
    A. Closer   B. No change   C. Less close

67. **Your school attendance:**
    A. Attendance improved   B. Stayed the same
    C. Attendance got worse   D. I dropped out

68. **Your partner's school attendance:**   A. Attendance improved
    B. Stayed the same   C. Attendance got worse   D. Partner dropped out

69. **College/Trade school plans:**
    A. More likely to attend   B. No change   C. Less likely to attend

70. Do you want your partner to continue his/her education?
    A. Absolutely   B. Probably   C. It doesn't matter
    D. Probably not   E. Absolutely not

71. Do you and your partner have enough money for your important needs?
    A. Absolutely   B. Most of the time   C. Some of the time
    D. Often we don't   E. We never have enough money

72. Do you and your partner agree on how you spend the money you have?
    A. Nearly always   B. Part of the time   C. Almost never

73. Has money — or the lack of it — been a problem in your relationship?
    A. Always   B. Most of the time   C. Sometimes
    D. Not often   E. Never

74. Has money — or the lack of it — been a greater problem than you
    expected?
    A. Yes, much greater   B. Yes, somewhat greater   C. No

75. How do you and your partner pay for the things you need?
    A. Man works   B. Woman works   C. Both of us work
    D. Welfare   E. Money from parents F. Other

76. In your relationship, who does most of the housekeeping?
    A. Woman only   B. Woman mostly   C. Both
    D. Man mostly   E. Man only   F. Neither
    G. Parent(s)   H. Other

77. If you have a child, do you and your partner agree on how to discipline him/her?
    A. Almost always   B. Part of the time   C. Almost never

In *your* relationship, who is mostly responsible for the following tasks?

78. **Earning money:**   A. Woman only   B. Woman mostly
    C. Both   D. Man only   E. Man mostly   F. Neither

79. **Deciding how money is spent:**   A. Woman only   B. Woman mostly
    C. Both   D. Man only   E. Man mostly   F. Neither

80. **Paying bills:**   A. Woman only   B. Woman mostly
    C. Both   D. Man only   E. Man mostly   F. Neither

81. **Vacuuming the house:**   A. Woman only   B. Woman mostly
    C. Both   D. Man only   E. Man mostly   F. Neither

82. **Mopping floors:**   A. Woman only   B. Woman mostly
    C. Both   D. Man only   E. Man mostly   F. Neither

83. **Preparing meals:**   A. Woman only   B. Woman mostly
    C. Both   D. Man only   E. Man mostly   F. Neither

84. **Cleaning up after meals:**   A. Woman only   B. Woman mostly
    C. Both   D. Man only   E. Man mostly   F. Neither

85. **Doing family laundry:**   A. Woman only   B. Woman mostly
    C. Both   D. Man only   E. Man mostly   F. Neither

86. **Washing the car:**   A. Woman only   B. Woman mostly
    C. Both   D. Man only   E. Man mostly   F. Neither

87. **Mowing the lawn:**   A. Woman only   B. Woman mostly
    C. Both   D. Man only   E. Man mostly   F. Neither

88. **Changing baby's diapers:**   A. Woman only   B. Woman mostly
    C. Both   D. Man only   E. Man mostly
    F. Neither   G. We don't have a child

89. **Feeding babies/children:**   A. Woman only   B. Woman mostly
    C. Both   D. Man only   E. Man mostly
    F. Neither   G. We don't have a child

90. **Bathing baby:**   A. Woman only   B. Woman mostly
    C. Both   D. Man only   E. Man mostly
    F. Neither   G. We don't have a child

91. **Putting baby to bed:**   A. Woman only   B. Woman mostly
    C. Both   D. Man only   E. Man mostly
    F. Neither   G. We don't have a child

92. **Putting toddler to bed:**   A. Woman only   B. Woman mostly
    C. Both   D. Man only   E. Man mostly
    F. Neither   G. We don't have a child

93. **Disciplining children:**   A. Woman only   B. Woman mostly
    C. Both   D. Man only   E. Man mostly
    F. Neither   G. We don't have a child

94. **Playing with the children:**   A. Woman only   B. Woman mostly
    C. Both   D. Man only   E. Man mostly
    F. Neither   G. We don't have a child

How would you rate your partner's abilities/actions in the following areas?

95. **Good money manager**: A. Excellent   B. Good   C. Fair   D. Poor

96. **Loves and cares about children:**   A. Excellent   B. Good
    C. Fair   D. Poor

97. **Good cook:**   A. Excellent   B. Good   C. Fair   D. Poor

98. **Good housekeeper:** A. Excellent   B. Good   C. Fair   D. Poor

99. **Makes plumbing and other repairs:**   A. Excellent   B. Good
    C. Fair   D. Poor

100. **Takes care of the yard:**   A. Excellent   B. Good   C. Fair   D. Poor

101. **Good sex partner:**   A. Excellent   B. Good   C. Fair   D. Poor

102. **Shares common interests with you:**   A. Excellent   B. Good
     C. Fair   D. Poor

103. **Spends most of his/her time with you:**   A. Excellent   B. Good
     C. Fair   D. Poor

104. When you're not in school, do you expect to work outside your home if
     you have no children?
     A. Yes   B. Probably   C. Probably not   D. Absolutely not

105. When s/he's not in school, do you expect your partner to work outside
     your home if you have no children?
     A. Yes   B. Probably   C. Probably not   D. Absolutely not

106. When you're not in school, do you expect to work outside your home if
     you have children under 2 years of age?
     A. Yes   B. Probably   C. Probably not   D. Absolutely not

107. When s/he's not in school, do you expect your partner to work outside your home if you have children under two years of age?
    A. Yes   B. Probably   C. Probably not   D. Absolutely not

108. Do you expect to work outside your home if you have children aged 2-5?
    A. Yes   B. Probably   C. Probably not   D. Absolutely not

109. Do you expect your partner to work outside your home if you have children aged 2-5?
    A. Yes   B. Probably   C. Probably not   D. Absolutely not

110. Do you expect to work outside your home if all the children are in school?
    A. Yes   B. Probably   C. Probably not   D. Absolutely not

111. Do you expect your partner to work outside your home if your children are in school?
    A. Yes   B. Probably   C. Probably not   D. Absolutely not

112. Is it all right for a man to tell his partner she must *not* work away from home?
    A. Yes   B. Probably   C. Probably not   D. Absolutely not

113. Is it all right for a man to tell his partner she *must* work away from home?
    A. Yes   B. Probably   C. Probably not   D. Absolutely not

114. Is it all right for a man to stay home while his partner gets a job?
    A. Yes   B. Probably   C. Probably not   D. Absolutely not

115. **MALES:** Are you jealous if your partner looks at other boys?
    FEMALES: Are you jealous if your partner looks at other girls?
    A. Absolutely   B. Usually   C. Sometimes
    D. Usually not   E. Absolutely not

116. **MALES:** Are you jealous if your partner talks with other boys?
    FEMALES: Are you jealous if your partner talks with other girls?
    A. Absolutely   B. Usually   C. Sometimes
    D. Usually not   E. Absolutely not

117. **MALES:** Are you jealous if your partner works with other boys?
    FEMALES: Are you jealous if your partner works with other girls?
    A. Absolutely   B. Usually   C. Sometimes
    D. Usually not   E. Absolutely not

118. **MALES:** Are you jealous if your partner goes to school with other boys?
    FEMALES: Are you jealous if your partner goes to school with other girls?
    A. Absolutely   B. Usually   C. Sometimes
    D. Usually not   E. Absolutely not

119. **MALES:** Would you be jealous if your partner went to a concert with
     another boy?
     FEMALES: Would you be jealous if your partner went to a concert with
     another girl?
     A. Absolutely   B. Usually   C. Sometimes
     D. Usually not   E. Absolutely not

120. **MALES:** Would you be jealous if your partner had a close male friend?
     FEMALES: Would you be jealous if your partner had a close female
     friend?
     A. Absolutely   B. Usually   C. Sometimes
     D. Usually not   E. Absolutely not

**FOR MALES *AND* FEMALES—OPEN-ENDED QUESTIONS: Please
answer on a separate sheet of paper, then attach it to your answer sheet.**

1. What do you feel you have given up because of your partnership?

2. What is the subject of most of your arguments? (Money? Household
   chores? In-laws? Recreation? Children? Or???)

3. When, where, and why do most of your arguments occur?

4. What effect has education — or the lack of it — had on your relationship?

5. What are the biggest problems in your partnership?

6. What is good about your partnership?

7. **If you are married,** why did you decide on marriage rather than living
   together?

   If you are not married, why did you decide not to marry when you
   started living together?

8. Do you think your partnership will last "forever"? Please comment.

9. What advice do you have for teenagers who are not yet married and/or
   living together?

Please add any comments you wish about any of the questions.

BIBLIOGRAPHY

Many books are available in which marriage in general is discussed. Several hundred titles are listed under "Marriage" in the current edition of *Books in Print*. Quite a few resources concerned with teenage pregnancy and parenthood have been published. However, there are very few books dealing directly with teenage marriage and/or teenage couples who live together. In fact, the same edition of *Books in Print* lists only four under "Teenage Marriage," all of which are included here.

The following bibliography includes the books mentioned in *Teenage Couples: Expectations and Reality*. Also listed are other books dealing with marriage in general, effect of the first child on the marriage, dealing with partner abuse, and other relevant topics.

Price quotes are from *Books in Print*, 1995. Because prices change so rapidly, however, and because publishers move, it is wise to call your local library reference department for an updated price and address before ordering a book. If you can't find a book you want in your bookstore, you can usually get it directly from the publisher. Enclose $3 for shipping in addition to the price of the book. See page 192 for an order form for Morning Glory Press publications.

The Alan Guttmacher Institute. *Sex and America's Teenagers.* 1994.
    88 pp. $30. The Alan Guttmacher Institute, 120 Wall Street, 21st
    Floor, New York, NY 10005.
    *Easy-to-read format with charts and text provides the latest information on
    the transition teenagers make from childhood to adulthood, trends in
    teenage sexual activity and contraceptive use, incidence and outcomes of
    sexually transmitted diseases and pregnancy, and the effects of program-
    matic and policy interventions on teenage sexual behavior.*

Ayer, Eleanor H. *Everything You Need to Know About Teen
    Marriage.* 1991. 64 pp. $13.95. The Rosen Publishing Group, Inc.,
    29 East 21st Street, New York, NY 10010. 800/237-9932.
    *From the Need to Know Library, this is a brief but rather comprehensive
    overview of teenage marriage.*

Belsky, Jay, Ph.D., and John Kelly. *The Transition to Parenthood: How
    a First Child Changes a Marriage.* 1995. 288 pp. $12.95. Dell
    Publishing Co. Inc., 1540 Broadway, New York, NY 10036.
    *Belsky chronicles the moving story of three typical couples who become
    first-time parents, what happens to their lives—and what ultimately happens
    to their marriages. Based on a study of 250 couples, the book discusses
    changes in a couple's life together after their child is born, and how they
    can make their marriage grow stronger.*

Bessell, Harold, Ph.D. *Romance with the Right Person: A Guide to
    Understanding True Love.* 1993. 147 pp. $9.95. New Horizon
    Books, 13626 Orchard Gate Road, Poway, CA 92064.
    619/679-8937.
    *Goal of the book is to give young people the essential skills they need to
    find, recognize, and maintain healthy love relationships. Simple
    questionnaire format.*

Colgrove, Melba, Harold Bloomfield, and Peter McWilliam. *How to
    Survive the Loss of a Love.* 1993. $5.95. Prelude Press, 8159 Santa
    Monica Boulevard, Los Angeles, CA 90046. 800/543-3101.
    *Daily affirmations, survival poems, and sayings for anyone who has lost
    someone special.*

Cowan, Carolyn Pape, and Philip A. Cowan. *When Partners Become
    Parents: The Big Life Change for Couples.* 1993. $13. BasicBooks,
    A Division of HarperCollins Publishers, Inc., 10 E. 53rd St., New
    York, NY 10022. 800/242-7737.

Based on a ten-year study of one hundred couples, this book charts the tumultuous changes that greet the arrival of a first child. Not directed to teen parents, but material is certainly relevant to very young parents as well as to older people.

Gale, Jay, and Sheila Church. *30 Days to a Happier Marriage.* 1992, 196 pp. Hardcover, $15.95. Longmeadow Press, 201 High Ridge Road, Stamford, CT 06904. 203/352-2648.
Simple lessons that can help a couple build a stronger, more stimulating relationship. Stresses learning to communicate more effectively.

Gottman, John, Ph.D. *Why Marriages Succeed or Fail: How to Make Yours Last.* 1995, 234 pp. $12. Simon & Schuster, Rockefeller Center, 1230 Avenue of the Americas, New York, NY 10020. 212/698-7000.
A practical guide to repairing the way wives and husbands relate to each other and removing the patterns that lead to divorce.

Gordon, Sol. *Why Love Is Not Enough.* 1990. 153 pp. $6.95. Adams Publishing, 260 Center Street, Holbrook, MA 02343-1074. 800/872-5627.
Offers practical advice on relationship building. A good book for teens ready to consider mature versus immature relationships. Portions could provide excellent material for class discussions.

Helton, Anne Stewart. *Relationships without Violence: A Curriculum for Adolescents.* 1987. Includes 10-minute video. $65. Signet. March of Dimes Birth Defects Foundation, Texas Gulf Coast Chapter, 3000 Weslayan, Suite 100, Houston, TX 77027. 713/623-2020.
Addresses battering as a problem that can occur between anyone's family members and acquaintances. Curriculum is designed to assist young people in understanding what battering is, how and why it happens, and how to maintain relationships free from battering. The male propensity for dominance is identified as a major cause of violence against women, but it is presented in this curriculum as a socialization issue rather than a moral weakness or inherent evil. This makes it easier for males in the class to relate to the concept of male domination and to modify their attitudes and future behavior toward women.The five-session curriculum is an excellent resource for classroom use.

Leman, Dr. Kevin. *Sex Begins in the Kitchen—Renewing Emotional and Physical Intimacy in Marriage.* 1992. $8. Dell Publishing Co., 1540 Broadway, New York, NY 10036-4094. 800/223-6834.

*While Dr. Leman is not writing specifically to teenage couples, his book is a
wonderful resource for couples of any age. It's interesting and easy to read.
His point that sex is an all-day affair based on the couple's total relationship is an important concept. He uses lots of examples from his experience
as a marriage and family counselor and in presenting Family Living
Seminars throughout the country. His writing style is witty. It's
a delightful book.*

Lindsay, Jeanne Warren. ***Do I Have a Daddy? A Story About a Single-
Parent Child****. 1991. 48 pp. Paper, $5.95; hardcover, $12.95. Free
study guide. Morning Glory Press, 6595 San Haroldo Way, Buena
Park, CA 90620. 714/828-1998.*
*A beautiful book for the child who has never met his/her father. A special
sixteen-page section offers suggestions to single mothers.*

_____. ***School-Age Parents: The Challenge of Three-Generation
Living****. 1990. 224 pp. Paper, $10.95; hardcover, $15.95. Teacher's
Guide/Study Guide, $2.50 set. Morning Glory Press.
*A much needed book for dealing with the frustrations, problems, and
pleasures of three-generation living. Useful for helping teen parents
communicate with **their** parents.*

_____. ***Teen Dads: Rights, Responsibilities and Joys****. 1993. 192 pp.
Paper, $9.95; hardcover, $15.95. Teacher's Guide and Workbook,
$2.50 each. Morning Glory Press.
*A how-to-parent book especially for teenage fathers. Offers help in
parenting from conception to age 3 of the child. Many quotes from and
photos of teen fathers.*

_____. ***Teenage Couples—Caring, Commitment and Change: How
to Build a Relationship that Lasts****. 1995. 208 pp. Paper, $9.95;
hardcover, $15.95. Workbook, $2.50. Curriculum Guide (also
includes **Teenage Couples—Coping with Reality)**, $19.95. Morning
Glory Press.
*Covers such important topics as communication, handling arguments,
keeping romance alive, sex in a relationship, jealousy, alcohol and drug
addiction, partner abuse, and divorce. Lots of quotes from teenage couples.*

_____. ***Teenage Couples—Coping with Reality: Dealing with
Money, In-laws, Babies and Other Details of Daily Life****. 1995. 192
pp. Paper, $9.95; hardcover, $15.95. Workbook, $2.50. Curriculum
Guide (see preceding notation). Morning Glory Press.
*Companion volume to **Teenage Couples—Caring, Commitment and
Change**. Good discussion, as the title implies, of the financial*

responsibilities of marriage and living together, living with in-laws, importance of education and job preparation, role-sharing, pregnancy, and parenting. Lots of quotes from teenage couples.

Marecek, Mary. ***Breaking Free from Partner Abuse.*** 1993. 96 pp. $7.95. Free study guide. Quantity discount. Morning Glory Press.
Lovely illustrations by Jami Moffett. Underlying message is that the reader does not deserve to be hit. Simply written. Can help a young woman escape an abusive relationship.

Sousa, Carole, ed. ***Preventing Teen Dating Violence: A Five-Session Curriculum for Teaching Adolescents.*** 1996. $50. ***Respect Can't Be Beat: Peer Leader's Manual.*** 1995. $15. Dating Violence Intervention Project, P.O. 530, Harvard Square Station, Cambridge, MA 02238. 617/354-2676.
Five-session curriculum with three components: Preventive education, intervention through school-based victim groups and perpetrator groups, and peer empowerment. Designed to be teen-taught with a male and a female leader. Curriculum is user friendly—includes all the information needed to present program. Good resource.

Musick, Judith S. ***Young, Poor, and Pregnant: The Psychology of Teenage Motherhood.*** 1995. 256 pp. $15. Yale University Press, 302 Temple Street, New Haven, CT 06511. 203/432-0960.
Musick, an expert on adolescent pregnancy, discusses how psychological pressures of adolescence interact with the problems of being poor to create a situation in which early sexuality, pregnancy, and childbearing—often repeated childbearing—seem almost inevitable.

Wallerstein, Judith S., and Sandra Blakeslee. ***The Good Marriage: How and Why Love Lasts.*** 1995. 384 pp. $24.95. Houghton Mifflin Company, 222 Berkeley Street, Boston, MA 02116, 617/351-5000.
Based on a study of 50 couples who consider themselves happily married, Wallerstein describes what she considers the four basic types of marriage: romantic, rescue, companionate, and traditional.

Weeks, John R. ***Teenage Marriages—A Demographic Analysis.*** 1976. 192 pp. $49.95. Greenwood Press, 88 Post Rd. W., Westport, CT 06881.
*Old research, but still the only such study listed in **Books in Print**. This is a detailed report of a study started in 1970 as part of a larger program of investigation into fertility and family formation at International Population and Urban Research (IPUR), University of California, Berkeley. It's a good discussion of teenage marriage in the United States including lots of statistics through 1973.*

ABOUT
THE AUTHOR

Jeanne Warren Lindsay has worked with hundreds of pregnant and parenting teenagers. She developed the Teen Parent Program at Tracy High School, Cerritos, California, in 1972, and coordinated the program for many years. She is the author of 15 other books dealing with adolescent pregnancy and parenting including the four-book *Teens Parenting* series used in many classrooms, and the other two books in the *Teenage Couples* series: *Teenage Couples—Caring, Commitment and Change* and *Teenage Couples—Coping with Reality.*

Lindsay grew up on a farm in Kansas. She has lived in the same house in Buena Park, California, for 35 years. She loves to visit the Middle West, but says she's now addicted to life in Southern California.

Lindsay has graduate degrees in Anthropology and Consumer and Family Science. She and Bob have five children and five grandchildren.

She is the editor of *PPT Express,* a quarterly newsletter for teachers and others working with pregnant and parenting teens. She speaks frequently at conferences across the country, but says she is happiest while interviewing young people for her books or writing under the big elm tree in her back yard.

INDEX

MORNING GLORY PRESS

6595 San Haroldo Way, Buena Park, CA 90620
714/828-1998 — FAX 714/828-2049

Please send me the following: Price   Total

Teenage Couples: Expectations and Reality
___   Paper, ISBN 0-930934-98-9   14.95 _____
___   Cloth, ISBN 0-930934-99-7   21.95 _____
   Teenage Couples: Caring, Commitment and Change
___   Paper, ISBN 0-930934-93-8   9.95 _____
___   Cloth, ISBN 0-930934-92-x   15.95 _____
  Teenage Couples: Coping with Reality
___   Paper, ISBN 0-930934-86-5   9.95 _____
___   Cloth, ISBN 0-930934-87-3   15.95 _____
___ **Beyond Dreams**   Paper, ISBN 1-885356-00-5   8.95 _____
___ **Too Soon for Jeff**   Paper, ISBN 0-930934-91-1   8.95 _____
___ **Detour for Emmy**   Paper, ISBN 0-930934-76-8   8.95 _____
___ **Telling**   Paper, ISBN 1-885356-03-x   8.95 _____
___ **Teen Dads**   Paper, ISBN 0-930934-78-4   9.95 _____
___ **Do I Have a Daddy?**   Cloth, ISBN 0-930934-45-8   12.95 _____
___ **Did My First Mother Love Me?** ISBN 0-930934-85-7   12.95 _____
___ **Breaking Free from Partner Abuse** 0-930934-74-1   7.95 _____
___ **Surviving Teen Pregnancy**   Paper, 1-885356-06-4   11.95 _____
  School-Age Parents: Three-Generation Living
___   Paper, ISBN 0-930934-36-9   10.95 _____
 Teens Parenting—Your Pregnancy and Newborn Journey
___   Paper, ISBN 0-930934-50-4   9.95 _____
___   Cloth, ISBN 0-930934-51-2   15.95 _____
  Easier Reading Edition—Pregnancy and Newborn Journey
___   Paper, ISBN 0-930934-61-x   9.95 _____
  Spanish—Adolescentes como padres—La jornada . . .
___   Paper, ISBN 0-930934-69-5   9.95 _____
  Teens Parenting—Your Baby's First Year
___   Paper, ISBN 0-930934-52-0   9.95 _____
  Teens Parenting—Challenge of Toddlers
___   Paper, ISBN 0-930934-58-x   9.95 _____
  Teens Parenting—Discipline from Birth to Three
___   Paper, ISBN 0-930934-54-7   9.95 _____
___ **VIDEO: "Discipline from Birth to Three"**   195.00 _____

___ **VIDEO: "Your Baby's First Year"**   195.00 _____

TOTAL   _____

Please add postage: 10% of total—Min., $3.00   _____
California residents add 7.75% sales tax

TOTAL   _____

Ask about quantity discounts, Teacher, Student Guides.
Prepayment requested. School/library purchase orders accepted.
If not satisfied, return in 15 days for refund.

NAME _____

ADDRESS _____

_____